HOBBES'S CHOICE RECIPES

A.C. (Andy) Caplet appears in these books by Wilkie Martin

Unhuman Series

Inspector Hobbes and the Blood
Inspector Hobbes and the Curse
Inspector Hobbes and the Gold Diggers
Inspector Hobbes and the Bones

Also by Wilkie Martin

Fiction

Razor

Poetry

Relative Disasters – A Little Book of Silly
Verse

And children's books, written as Wilkie J. Martin

All in the Same Boat
The Lazy Rabbit

HOBBES'S CHOICE RECIPES

How to cook the Sorenchester way,
with Mrs Goodfellow's very best everyday recipes

COLLECTED BY

A.C. CAPLET

The Witcherley Book Company
United Kingdom

Published in United Kingdom
by The Witcherley Book Company in 2019

First published in 2019

British Library Cataloguing in Publication Data. A catalogue record for this book is available from the British Library.

ISBN 9781912348367 (paperback)
ISBN 9781912348374 (kindle)
ISBN 9781912348381 (epub)
ISBN 9781912348398 (hardback)

Contents

Introduction

Inspector Hobbes is a character in the *Unhuman* series of comedy cosy mystery fantasies by Wilkie Martin.
Mrs Goodfellow is Hobbes's housekeeper and A.C. (Andy) Caplet, the narrator in the books, is a failed newspaper reporter reinvented as a food critic. All the books in the *Unhuman* series mention food, much of it cooked by Mrs Goodfellow who, according to Andy, is a wonderful cook.

Due to popular demand (well, one person asked!), Wilkie wanted to produce a Mrs Goodfellow cookbook. Whenever he (or his partner) cooked something, the question was asked, *'is it good enough for Mrs G?'* If yes, the recipe was recorded. Now with over one hundred, they have been compiled in this little book.

These recipes reflect actual meals that Wilkie Martin either cooked or ate. They were collected during the writing of *Inspector Hobbes and the Gold Diggers*, *Inspector Hobbes and the Bones*, and *Razor*. As Wilkie and his partner were on various diets for some of the time, a few recipes reflect their way of eating at the time.

These recipes are presented as having been collected by A.C. Caplet from his observations. They are ones he would think nearly good enough to accredit to Mrs G and he hopes you enjoy them. He thinks, though, that they lack her magic touch.

Note. All meals are for two people unless otherwise indicated.

SOUP

1 Butternut Squash Soup

Ingredients	Quantity	Preparation
Bouillon powder	2-3 teaspoons	
Butternut squash	1 medium	Deseeded and quartered
Chicken stock	1litre/2pints	
Chillies (red or green)	1	Chopped
Fresh garlic	1 clove	Chopped
Olive oil	1+2 tablespoons	
Onion	1	Chopped
Parmesan cheese	50g/1.75oz/1/3cup	Cubed - small

In a roasting pan, and a large pan or pressure cooker.
1. Rub the cut sides of the butternut squash with 1 tablespoon of olive oil and roast at Gas Mark 6/Electric 200°c/Fan 180°c for 45 minutes (or microwave for 15 minutes).
2. In the large pan or pressure cooker, heat 2 tablespoons of olive oil and fry the onions until soft.
3. Add fresh garlic and chillies, and fry gently for 2 minutes.
4. Add the chicken stock and bring to a simmer.
5. Scoop out the butternut squash flesh, add to the chicken stock and stir well.
6. When boiling, add any chicken bits retrieved from the carcass when making the stock and blend.
7. Add cubes of Parmesan cheese.
8. Add bouillon powder to taste and stir in well.
9. Serve.

2 Creamed Curried Marrow Soup

Ingredients	Quantity	Preparation
Bouillon powder	4 teaspoons	
Double cream	3 tablespoon	
Dried rosemary	3-4 teaspoons	
Fresh garlic	2 cloves	Crushed and chopped
Green marrow	1 large	Quartered and deseeded
Ground almonds	100g/3.5oz/0.7cup	
Mild curry powder	4 teaspoons	
Olive oil	4+2 tablespoons	
Parmesan cheese	50g/1.75oz/1/3cup	Cubed
Red onion	½	Diced
Water	1litre/2pints	Boiling

In roasting pan and a large pan.

1. Cover the green marrow with the 4 tablespoons of olive oil.
2. Roast the green marrow on Gas Mark 8/Electric 230°c/Fan 210°c for 45 minutes (or microwave for 15 minutes).
3. In the large pan, heat 2 tablespoons of olive oil. Add red onion and fresh garlic, and fry for 3 minutes.
4. Remove roasted green marrow flesh from the skin and dice.
5. Add dried rosemary and mild curry powder to the red onion and continue to fry until you can smell the spices.
6. Add ground almonds and stir in.
7. Add diced green marrow, boiling water, bouillon powder and boil for 10 minutes.
8. Add diced cubes of Parmesan cheese and double cream.
9. Serve.

3 Creamy Cauliflower Soup

Ingredients	Quantity	Preparation
Cauliflower	350g/12oz/2.3cup	
Fresh garlic	2 cloves	Crushed and chopped
Mild curry powder	1.5 teaspoons	
Olive oil	1 tablespoon	
Red chillies	1 small	Chopped
Red lentils	100g/3.5oz/0.7cup	
Soft cream cheese	100g/3.5oz/0.7cup	
Vegetable stock	1litre/2pints	

In a large pan.
1. Break cauliflower into small florets and put into a food processor and blitz to small grains to make cauliflower rice.
2. Heat the olive oil. Add the red lentils, fresh garlic and red chillies, mix well and fry for 2 minutes until lentils change colour.
3. Add mild curry powder, and fry for a further 1 to 2 minutes until you can smell the spices.
4. Add cauliflower and mix well.
5. Add vegetable stock and bring to a simmer for 10 to 15 minutes.
6. Add soft cream cheese. Mix well and stir until soft cream cheese is melted.
7. Serve.

4 Leftover Cream Chilli Chicken Butternut Soup

Ingredients	Quantity	Preparation
Bouillon powder	3 teaspoons	
Butternut squash	½	Peeled, deseeded and diced
Chilli-infused olive oil	2 tablespoons	
Double cream	2 tablespoons	
Fresh garlic	3 cloves	Crushed and chopped
Green chillies	1	Diced
Leftover cooked roast chicken carcass	1	
Onion	1	Diced
Water	1litre/2pints	

In a pressure cooker or a large pan.

1. Fry the onion, green chillies, fresh garlic in chilli-infused olive oil.
2. Add leftover cooked roast chicken carcass in a trivet. Add water and boil or pressure cook for 30 minutes to 1 hour.
3. Remove chicken carcass and any loose bones. Sieve if necessary.
4. Add butternut squash and bring back to the boil, and cook the squash for 10 minutes until soft.
5. Strip any remaining chicken meat from the carcass then add it back to the soup.
6. Add bouillon powder to taste and blend the mixture until smooth.
7. Add double cream and serve.

5 Mrs G's Onion Soup

Ingredients	Quantity	Preparation
Chicken stock	1litre/2pints	
Coconut oil	2 tablespoons	
Fresh garlic	4 cloves	Crushed and chopped
Fresh ginger	4cm/1.5in	Chopped finely
Green chillies	1	Chopped finely
Olive oil	1 tablespoon	
Onion	½	Chopped finely
Parmesan cheese	50g/1.75oz/1/3cup	Cubed
Spanish onion	1 large	Chopped finely

In a large pan.

1. Heat the coconut oil with the olive oil, and when melted add the onion and Spanish onion and fry until translucent, 10 minutes.

2. Add fresh garlic, fresh ginger and green chillies and continue to fry until the onions start to brown, 5 minutes.

3. Add chicken stock and let simmer for 5 minutes.

4. Add cubes of Parmesan cheese and wait for it to melt before serving.

5. Serve with crusty bread.

6 Pigeon Leftovers with Vegetable Soup

Ingredients	Quantity	Preparation
Bouillon powder	4-5 teaspoons	
Celery	4 sticks	
Chilli powder	Pinch	
Courgette	1 large	Chopped
Cumin powder	1 teaspoon	
Fresh garlic	6 cloves	Crushed and chopped
Green cabbage leaves	4 large	Chopped
Leek	½ large	Chopped
Olive oil	1+2 tablespoons	
Onion	1 large	Chopped
Leftover roast pigeon carcasses	2	Roasted, breast removed and used for alternative dish
Tomato	2	Chopped
Water	1litre/2pints	Boiling
Worcestershire sauce	Dash	

In a pressure cooker.
1. Fry onion, fresh garlic and celery in olive oil for 5 minutes.
2. Add the leftover roast pigeon carcasses in a trivet. (If not already roasted then roast them first: rub the pigeons in oil and roast for 20 minutes, Gas Mark 5/Electric 190°c/Fan 170°c. Remove breasts and use for another meal.)
3. Pour boiling water on the previously roasted carcasses.
4. Put lid on pressure cooker, bring to pressure and cook for 20 minutes.
5. Reduce pressure and remove pigeon carcasses. Add remaining vegetables (green cabbage leaves, courgettes, leeks and tomatoes) and put lid back on.
6. Pick meat off pigeon carcasses (including any bits of liver, etc., taking care to avoid bones and any shot pellets).
7. Blend the soup, adding the cumin powder, chilli powder and bouillon powder.
8. Add picked pigeon meat and a dash of Worcestershire sauce.
9. Heat in pressure cooker, bring up to pressure.
10. Cook for 5 minutes. Reduce pressure and serve.

Note. If not pressure cooking, cook in large covered pan for longer (about 1.5 times longer).

7 Pigeon Mulligatawny Soup

Ingredients	Quantity	Preparation
Bouillon powder	4 tablespoons	
Cabbage leaves	2 leaves	Shredded
Celeriac	250g/9oz/1.7cup	Diced
Coconut oil	1 tablespoon	
Curry powder	2-3 teaspoons	
Fresh coriander	Bunch	
Fresh garlic	2 cloves	Crushed and chopped
Fresh ginger	2.5cm/1in	Chopped small
Ground almonds	3 tablespoons	
Lemon juice	2 teaspoons	
Mustard seeds	1 teaspoon	
Onion	1	Chopped
Pigeon breasts	2	Chopped
Pigeon stock	750ml/1.5pint	
Tomato	1	Chopped

In a frying pan and large covered pan.

1. Fry the mustard seeds in coconut oil until they pop.
2. Add onion, fresh garlic and fresh ginger and fry until onion is translucent.
3. Add curry powder and fry for 1 minute.
4. Add tomato, crush and fry to a paste.
5. In the large pan, heat up pigeon stock with remaining vegetables (cabbage leaves and celeriac) and bring to a simmer. Add pigeon breasts and ground almonds.
6. When simmering, add onion and spice mix and bouillon powder.
7. Simmer until vegetables are tender.
8. Blend until an even consistency.
9. Add fresh coriander and lemon juice and serve.

Note. Can be served over Basmati rice – place a spoonful or two of cooked Basmati rice in your bowl then add the soup.

8 Spiced Butternut Soup

Ingredients	Quantity	Preparation
Butternut squash	1	Deseeded and quartered
Chicken stock	1litre/2pints	
Desiccated coconut	1 tablespoon	
Fresh garlic	3 cloves	Crushed and chopped
Green chillies	2	Chopped
Ground almonds	2 tablespoons	
Lettuce leaves	Handful	Chopped
Olive oil	1+1 tablespoon	
Onion	1	Chopped finely
Paprika powder	1 teaspoon	
Parmesan cheese	To taste	Cubed
Tomato	1	Chopped
Turmeric powder	1 teaspoon	

In a roasting pan and a large pan.

1. Rub the butternut squash with 1 tablespoon of olive oil and roast in the oven at Gas Mark 6/Electric 200°c/Fan 180°c for 45 minutes until soft (or microwave for 15 minutes).

2. Tip the remaining oil from roasting pan once roasted plus 1 tablespoon of olive oil into the large pan (add more if required) then fry the onion, fresh garlic and green chillies until soft.

3. Add tomato, crush and fry to a paste.

4. Add turmeric powder and paprika powder and fry for 2 minutes.

5. Add ground almonds and stir in.

6. Add chicken stock and bring to the boil, then simmer.

7. Remove and add butternut squash flesh.

8. Cook for 5 minutes and then blend.

9. Add tiny cubes of Parmesan cheese and lettuce leaves and stir in.

10. Serve with desiccated coconut, to taste.

9 Spiced Butternut Squash and Mushroom Soup

Ingredients	Quantity	Preparation
Butternut squash	Small	Deseeded and quartered
Fresh garlic	2 cloves	Crushed and chopped
Fresh ginger	2.5cm/1in	Chopped
Ground almonds	2-3 tablespoons	
Leek	½	Diced
Onion	½	Chopped
Mushrooms	250g/9oz/1.7cup	Chopped
Parmesan cheese	To taste	Grated
Rapeseed oil	1+1 tablespoon	
Red chillies	1 small	Chopped
Stock	1litre/2pints	
Turmeric powder	1 teaspoon	

In a roasting pan and large pan.

1. Rub cut sides of butternut squash with 1 tablespoon of olive oil.
2. Roast in oven Gas Mark 6/Electric 200°c/Fan 180°c for 1 hour or until soft (or microwave for 15 minutes).
3. In the large pan, fry onion, fresh garlic, fresh ginger, leeks and red chillies in 1 tablespoon of rapeseed oil until onion starts browning.
4. Add mushrooms and cook for 5 minutes.
5. Add turmeric powder, mix and cook for 2 to 3 minutes.
6. Take butternut squash flesh from skin and add to mixture.
7. Add stock and ground almonds and bring to the boil. Add grated Parmesan cheese.
8. Simmer for 10 minutes.
9. Serve with fresh crusty bread.

10 Spiced Chicken Soup

Ingredients	Quantity	Preparation
Carrot	1	Chopped
Celery	1 stick	Chopped
Chicken stock	750ml/1.5pints	
Chicken thighs	250g/9oz/1.7cup	Skinned and cut small
Chillies (red or green)	1 (or to taste)	Chopped
Coconut oil	1 tablespoon	
Courgette	1	Chopped
Double cream	Dollop	
Fennel seeds	1 teaspoon	
Fresh garlic	3	Chopped
Lettuce	Few leaves	Chopped
Onion	1	Chopped
Paprika powder	1 teaspoon	
Sweet red pepper	1	Chopped
Tomato	1	Chopped
Turmeric powder	1 teaspoon	

In a large pan.
1. Fry onion, fresh garlic and chillies in coconut oil.
2 Add chicken thighs and fry until chicken starts to brown.
3. Add vegetables (carrots, celery, courgettes, tomatoes and, sweet red pepper) and stir in.
4. Add spices (fennel seeds, paprika powder and turmeric powder) and chicken stock and stir in.
5. Bring to boil and simmer for 15 minutes.
6. Add finely chopped lettuce.
7. Add a dollop of double cream and blend in.
8. Serve.

11 Spicy Lamb Soup

Ingredients	Quantity	Preparation
Cabbage leaves	2-3	Chopped
Chilli powder	½ teaspoon	
Fresh garlic	1 clove	Chopped
Lamb stock	1litre/2pints	
Olive oil	2 tablespoons	
Onion	1	Chopped
Paprika powder	1 teaspoon	
Sweet pepper (any)	½	Chopped
Tomato	1	Chopped
Turmeric powder	½ teaspoon	

In a large pan.

1. Heat 2 tablespoons of olive oil and fry onion and fresh garlic until onion is brown.

2. Add chilli powder and turmeric powder and fry for 2 minutes.

3. Add paprika powder and tomato, crush and cook until tomato makes a paste.

4. Add cabbage leaves and sweet pepper and stir in.

5. Add lamb stock (with bones removed) and bring to the boil and simmer for 10 minutes.

6. Serve.

12 Spicy Miso Crab Soup

Ingredients	Quantity	Preparation
Butter	2 tablespoons	
Chillies (red or green)	2 small	Cut finely
French beans	8	Diced small
Fresh garlic	4 cloves	Crushed and chopped
Fresh ginger	2.5cm/1in	Cut finely
Ground coriander	2 teaspoons	
Ground dried rosemary	1 teaspoon	Ground
Leek	½	Cut finely
Miso soup paste	2 packs, 2 * 15g/0.5oz/0.1cup	
Oil	2 tablespoons	
Onion	½	Cut finely
Tin crab meat	340g/12oz/2.25cup	Drained
Water	1litre/2pints	Boiling

In a large pan.
1. Heat oil and add onion and cook to soften.
2. Add fresh garlic, chillies and fresh ginger and fry for 2 to 3 minutes.
3. Add ground coriander, butter and ground dried rosemary.
4. When butter has melted add leeks and French beans.
5. When leeks have softened, drain and add the tinned crab meat and mix well.
6. Add water and Miso soup paste. Stir well and warm through for 3 minutes.
7. Serve.

13 Two Fish Soup

Ingredients	Quantity	Preparation
Bouillon powder	3 teaspoons	
Coconut oil	1 tablespoon	
Courgette	1 large	Diced
Fresh garlic	2 cloves	Crushed and chopped
Ground black pepper	2 teaspoons	
Onion	½	Diced
Savoy cabbage	100g/3.5oz/0.7cup	Diced
Smoked haddock or other smoked white fish	200g/7oz/1.3cup	Skinned and diced
Water	1litre/2pints	Boiling
Cod or coley or other white fish	350g/12oz/2.3cup	Skinned and diced

In a wok or a large pan.
1. Heat coconut oil and fry onions until translucent.
2. Add fresh garlic and fry.
3. Add courgettes and savoy cabbage and fry to soften.
4. Add cod, coley or other white fish and smoked haddock or other smoked white fish, water, ground black pepper and bouillon powder and stir.
5. Bring to boil and allow to simmer for 5 minutes.
6. Serve.

SALAD

14 Diet Egg Salad

Ingredients	Quantity	Preparation
Celery	3 sticks	Diced small
Cucumber	½	Diced
Eggs	3-4	Boiled and diced
Ground black pepper	1 teaspoon	
Red wine vinegar	1 tablespoon	
Romaine lettuce	½	Diced
Salt	Pinch	
Turmeric powder	¼ teaspoon	

In a salad bowl.
1. Mix the diced cucumber with the salt, red wine vinegar and ground black pepper and leave for 2 to 3 minutes.
2. Add the celery and romaine lettuce and mix well.
3. Add turmeric powder and mix well.
4. Add the egg and stir through, trying not to break up the egg too much.
5. Serve.

Note. Add cheese if feeling peckish.

15 Diet Pepper Tuna Salad

Ingredients	Quantity	Preparation
Celery	3 sticks	Diced small
Cucumber	½	Diced
Ground black pepper	1 teaspoon	
Red wine vinegar	½ tablespoon	
Romaine lettuce	½	Diced
Salt	Pinch	
Tin tuna	150g/5.25oz/1cup	Drained and flaked

In a salad bowl.
1. Flake the tuna into the bowl.
2. Add the diced cucumber, salt and ground black pepper and red wine vinegar and mix well. Leave for 5 minutes.
3. Add celery and romaine lettuce and mix well.
4. Serve.

16 Fried Chicken Salad

Ingredients	Quantity	Preparation
Chicken breasts	200g/7oz/1.3cup	Diced
Chilli-infused olive oil	2 teaspoons	
Crème fraîche	50g/1.75oz/0.3cup	
Dried mustard powder	¼ teaspoon	
Dried walnuts	60g/2oz/0.4cup	Chopped
Ground fenugreek	¼ teaspoon	
Pea shoots	2 handfuls	Chopped
Rocket leaves	2 handfuls	Chopped
Sunflower oil	3 tablespoon	
Turmeric powder	1 teaspoon	

In a salad bowl and a frying pan.

1. Put the rocket and pea shoots in the salad bowl.

2. In the frying pan, heat sunflower oil and chilli-infused olive oil and add spices (dried mustard powder, ground fenugreek and turmeric powder).

3. Add and fry chicken breast until it starts to brown.

4. Add dried walnuts and fry for a further 1 to 2 minutes.

5. Stir through crème fraîche.

6. Add to salad bowl and mix well.

7. Serve.

17 Leftover Roast Beef Salad

Ingredients	Quantity	Preparation
Celery	1 stick	Diced
Cos lettuce	½	Shredded
Cox apples or other eating apple	1 small	Cored and diced
Cucumber	7cm/3in	Diced
Leftover cooked roast beef brisket	200g/7oz/1.3cup	Shredded
Sweet red pepper	½ small	Sliced thinly
Salad Dressing		
Horseradish sauce	3 teaspoons	
Mayonnaise	1 tablespoon	
Rapeseed oil	2 tablespoons	

In a jug and a salad bowl.
1. Make the salad dressing in the jug: mix horseradish sauce, rapeseed oil and mayonnaise until oil emulsifies.
2. Mix other ingredients (celery, Cox apple or other eating apple, cucumber, leftover cooked beef brisket, cos lettuce and sweet red pepper) then stir through the salad dressing.
3. Serve.

18 Leftover Roast Chicken and Walnut Salad

Ingredients	Quantity	Preparation
Celery	2 sticks	Chopped
Cherry tomatoes	4	Halved
Cucumber	5cm/2in	Chopped
Dried walnuts	100g/3.5oz/0.7cup	Chopped
Leftover cooked chicken	200g/7oz/1.3cup	Diced
Rocket or dark green salad leaves	Handful	Chopped
Romaine lettuce or light green salad leaves	Handful	Chopped
Spring onions	1 large	Chopped
Salad Dressing		
Cider vinegar	2 teaspoons	
Garlic-infused olive oil	2.5 tablespoon	

In a jug and a salad bowl.
1. Make the salad dressing in the jug: mix garlic-infused olive oil and cider vinegar until oil emulsifies.
2. Mix all other ingredients (celery, cherry tomatoes, cucumber, rocket or dark green salad leaves, leftover cooked chicken, romaine lettuce or light green salad leaves, spring onions and dried walnuts) in bowl and add the salad dressing, mix well.
3. Serve.

19 Roast Pigeon Salad

Ingredients	Quantity	Preparation
Chinese leaf	½ a head	Chopped
Cucumber	1/3	Chopped
Olive oil	1 tablespoon	
Pigeon breasts	2	Roasted and allowed to cool
Pointy white cabbage or other white cabbage	2 leaves	Chopped
Spring onions	1	Chopped
Tomato	1	Chopped
Salad Dressing		
Extra virgin olive oil	3 teaspoons	
Mayonnaise	3 teaspoons	
White wine vinegar	1 teaspoon	

In a roasting pan, a jug and salad bowl.

1. Rub pigeons in olive oil and roast at Gas Mark 5/Electric 190°c/Fan 170°c for 20 minutes, allow to cool.
2. Make the salad dressing in the jug: mix mayonnaise, extra virgin olive oil and white wine vinegar into an emulsion.
3 Mix up all other ingredients (Chinese leaf, cucumber, spring onion, tomato and pointy white cabbage or other white cabbage), excluding the pigeon breasts.
4. Add salad dressing and toss.
5. Remove breasts from pigeons.
6. Remove skin and slice thinly. Add to salad.
7. Mix up and serve.

Note. The remaining pigeon carcasses can then be used to make stock or soup.

VEGETABLES

20 Celeriac Dauphinoise

Ingredients	Quantity	Preparation
Butter	Knob	
Celeriac	½ root	Cut into thin slices
Double cream	200ml/1/3pint	
Fresh garlic	2-3 cloves	Chopped
Onion	½	Chopped

In an oven pan.
1. Grease pan with butter.
2. Add a thin layer of onion and fresh garlic.
3. Add layer of celeriac and coat with double cream.
4. Continue building up layers.
5. Pour remaining cream on top.
6. Cook in oven Gas Mark 6/Electric 200°c/Fan 180°c for 1 hour.
7. Serve with Cajun Style Pheasant, roast meat or steak.

Note. Can precook celeriac by boiling or microwaving to save time then assemble and cook in oven for 20 minutes.

21 Chilli Vegetables

Ingredients	Quantity	Preparation
Aubergine	1 large	Cut into strips and diced
Coconut oil	2 tablespoons	
Green chillies	1	Diced
Groundnut oil	1 teaspoon	
Leek	1 medium	Chopped
Onion	1 small	Chopped

In a wok or frying pan.

1. Heat the coconut oil and groundnut oil together.

2. Add onion, leeks and green chillies and fry for 2 to 3 minutes.

3. Add aubergine and continue to fry, stirring it all together for 10 minutes.

4. Serve.

22 Creamed Mushrooms

Ingredients	Quantity	Preparation
Butter	Knob	
Double cream	1 tablespoon	
Fresh garlic (optional)	1-2 cloves	Crushed and chopped
Mushrooms	250g/9oz/1.7cup	Cut into large chunks
Soy sauce	Dash	
Soya milk or milk or water	Splash, if required	

In a saucepan.
1. Melt butter.
2. Add mushrooms and fresh garlic (if wanted), stir.
3. Cook on low heat, covered for 20 minutes, stirring occasionally, and adding a splash of soya milk, milk or water if it gets dry.
4. Stir in soy sauce.
5. Add double cream and stir in.
6. Take off heat for 1 minute.
7. Serve with fried bacon or baked sausages.

23 Creamy Curried Cauliflower

Ingredients	Quantity	Preparation
Bacon fat or oil	1 tablespoon	
Cauliflower	500g/17.5oz/3.3cup	Destemmed, broken into florets and chopped
Curry powder	2 teaspoons	
Leek	200g/7oz/1.3cup	Chopped finely
Red chillies	1	Diced small
Red onion	1 small	Chopped
Soft cream cheese	150g/5.25oz/1cup	
Soya milk or milk	4 tablespoons	

In a roasting pan, and a wok or a large pan.

1. Put cauliflower florets and soya milk or milk into roasting pan and put in oven Gas Mark 8/Electric 230°c/Fan 210°c to start warming.

2. Heat bacon fat or oil in wok or large pan and fry red onion, leeks and red chillies until they start to soften.

3. Add curry powder and mix well. Take off heat as soon as you can smell spices.

4. Take cauliflower out of oven.

5. Mix soft cream cheese into the onion, leeks and chilli mixture.

6. Cover the cauliflower with the cheesy spicy mixture.

7. Return to oven and cook for a further 30 to 40 minutes until cauliflower softens, stirring and turning every 10 to 15 minutes.

8. Serve.

24 Fresh Garlic, Fennel and Leeks

Ingredients	Quantity	Preparation
Coconut oil	1 tablespoon	
Fennel bulb	1 large	Cut in half and thinly sliced
Fresh garlic	4 cloves	Crushed and chopped
Leek	1 small	Cut in half lengthwise and thinly sliced
Sunflower oil	2 tablespoons	

In a wok or a frying pan.
1. Heat coconut oil and sunflower oil, add fennel bulb slices, leeks and fresh garlic, tossing in the oil.
2. Fry until fennel softens, 10 minutes.
3. Serve.

25 Fried Almond Courgettes

Ingredients	Quantity	Preparation
Courgettes	2 large	Sliced diagonally
Eggs	1 large	Beaten
Ground almonds	50g/1.75oz/0.3cup	
Oil	2-3 tablespoons	
Turmeric powder	2 teaspoons	

In 2 bowls, and a frying pan.
1. Slice the courgettes thickly diagonally.
2. Mix turmeric powder with the ground almonds in a bowl.
3. Dip the cut courgettes in beaten egg in a separate bowl.
4. Turn the courgettes in the almond mixture and drop into warmed oil in pan.
5. Heat oil and fry the egg and almond covered courgettes for 2 to 3 minutes before turning and frying other side for 2 to 3 minutes.
6. Serve.

26 Garlic Soft Cheese Dumplings with Roast Tomatoes

Ingredients	Quantity	Preparation
Bicarbonate of soda	¼ teaspoon	
Cherry tomatoes	200g/7oz/1.3cup	
Egg white powder	1 tablespoon	
Fresh basil	Handful	Shredded
Garlic-infused olive oil	3 tablespoons	
Ground almonds	100g/3.5oz/0.7cup	
Herby cheese roulade	200g/7oz/1.3cup	

In a bowl and a roasting pan.

1. Mix egg white powder and ground almonds in the bowl.

2. Add herby cheese roulade and bicarbonate of soda and mix well.

3. Using teaspoon, spoon out mixture and roll into balls. Place in roasting pan with a little of the garlic-infused olive oil.

4. Add the cherry tomatoes and scatter around the dumplings.

5. Pour garlic-infused olive oil over them and roll the dumplings and tomatoes in it.

6. Bake at Gas Mark 6/Electric 200°c/Fan 180°c for 15 minutes.

7. Turn dumplings and scatter fresh basil over and mix in. Return to oven for 10 minutes.

8 Before serving halve the cherry tomatoes and cut dumplings into 4, rolling it all in the remaining garlicky tomato sauce from the pan.

9. Serve.

27 Garlic Spinach

Ingredients	Quantity	Preparation
Double cream	Dollop	
Fresh garlic	1 clove	Chopped
Oil	1 tablespoon	
Spinach	200g/7oz/1.3cup	

In a large pan.
1. Heat oil and fry chopped fresh garlic for 1 to 2 minutes.
2. Add spinach and cook until wilted, about 1 minute.
3. Add a dash of double cream and stir in.
4. Serve with Baked Sea Bass.

28 Mock Chestnut or Garlic Butternut Squash

Ingredients	Quantity	Preparation
Butternut squash	1 small	Peeled, deseeded and cut into small cubes
Coconut oil	1 tablespoon	
Fresh garlic	3 cloves	Crushed and chopped
Groundnut or sunflower oil	1 tablespoon	
Red chillies	½ large	Sliced finely
Thick double cream	1 tablespoon	
Water	To cover	

In a large pan, and a wok or frying pan.
1. Boil the butternut squash for 10 to 15 minutes until it feels soft when tested with a knife.
2. Drain the butternut squash. (Save the water for Leftover Roast Beef Spicy with Radish, if doing together.)
3. In the wok or frying pan, heat the coconut oil and groundnut oil or sunflower oil together.
4. When coconut oil is melted, add red chillies and fresh garlic, and fry for 2 to 3 minutes.
5. Add the butternut squash and turn frequently. Fry for 5 minutes until squash just starts to brown.
6. Add the thick double cream and stir in well.
7. Serve with Leftover Roast Beef Spicy with Radish.

29 Mrs G's Leeks, Brussels Sprouts and Courgettes

Ingredients	Quantity	Preparation
Brussels sprouts	12 good sized	Shredded and blanched
Courgettes	1-2	Chopped
Dijon mustard	1 teaspoon	
Leek	1 small	Sliced
Rapeseed oil (or butter or olive oil)	1 tablespoon	
Water	To cover	Boiling

In a large pan.
1. Heat up rapeseed oil, butter or olive oil and leeks and cook on a low heat, stirring occasionally.
2. After 5 minutes, add courgettes and stir.
3. Blanch then add the Brussels sprouts.
4. Cook for 20 minutes, or until soft. Do not let brown.
5. Stir in 1 tablespoon Dijon mustard.
6. Serve with meat.

Note. Ideal accompaniment for a good juicy rib-eye steak.

30 Spiced Cauliflower

Ingredients	Quantity	Preparation
Cauliflower	1 medium	Broken into florets
Chillies (red or green)	1	Chopped finely
Cumin seeds	1 teaspoon	
Fresh garlic	3 cloves	Crushed and chopped
Mustard seeds	1 teaspoon	
Oil	1 tablespoon	
Onion	1	Chopped small
Smoked paprika powder	1 teaspoon	
Tomato	1 large	Chopped
Turmeric powder	1 teaspoon	
Water	To cover & splash	

In a wok or large pan, a pan and a roasting pan.

1. Pre-cook the cauliflower florets by boiling or microwaving in a pan until they start to soften.

2. While cauliflower cooks, using the wok or large pan, fry the onion in the oil until it is translucent.

3. Add fresh garlic and chillies and fry for further 1 to 2 minutes.

4. Add the rest of spices (cumin seeds, mustard seeds, smoked paprika powder and turmeric powder) and cook until the spices can be smelt.

5. Add tomato, crush and fry until it becomes a paste.

6. Put cauliflower florets into roasting pan with a little of the water.

7. Pour the sauce over the cauliflower and mix in.

8. Cook in oven, Gas Mark 5/Electric 190°c/Fan 170°c for 30 minutes or until cauliflower is soft enough to eat.

9. Serve.

MEAT

31 Almost Satay Beef

Ingredients	Quantity	Preparation
Chilli sauce	2 tablespoons	For marinade
Courgette	1	Peeled and diced
Dark soy sauce	1 tablespoon	For marinade
Fresh garlic	2 cloves	Crushed and chopped
Fresh ginger	1.25cm/½in	Diced
Leek	½	Cut into thin strips lengthwise
Peanut butter, crunchy	2 tablespoons	
Red onion	½	Chopped
Sirloin beef steak	500g/17.5oz/3.3cup	Remove excess fat and cut into strips
Sunflower oil	3 tablespoons	

In a bowl and a wok or a large pan.

1. Marinate sirloin beef in dark soy sauce and chilli sauce.
2. In the wok or large pan, heat the sunflower oil and add red onion, fresh garlic and fresh ginger. Fry until onion is translucent.
3. Add crunchy peanut butter and stir to make thick sauce.
4. Remove beef from marinade with slotted spoon and add to pan, turning to cook until browned.
5. Add leeks and courgettes and any remaining marinade, and mix well.
6. Cook altogether for 3 to 4 minutes until courgette is softened.
7. Serve with green salad.

32 Beanless Chilli Beef

Ingredients	Quantity	Preparation
Bouillon powder	3 teaspoons	
Chilli powder	½ teaspoon	
Cumin powder	2 teaspoons	
Fresh garlic	4 cloves	Crushed and chopped
Minced beef	500g/17.5oz/3.3cup	
Olive oil	2 tablespoons	
Parmesan cheese	20g/1oz/0.13cup	Ground
Red chillies	1 small	Chopped
Red onion	½	Chopped finely
Sweet orange or yellow pepper	1	Chopped
Tin chopped tomatoes	400g/14oz/2.6cup	
Tomato purée	1 tablespoon	
Water or stock	½ tomato tin	

In a pressure cooker or a large pan.

1. Fry the red onion in olive oil until translucent.

2. Add fresh garlic, sweet orange or yellow pepper and red chillies and fry for 2 to 3 minutes.

3. Add chilli powder and cumin powder, mix well, and fry until you can smell the spices.

4. Add minced beef and fry to brown.

5. Add bouillon powder and tomato purée and mix in well.

6. Add tin chopped tomatoes and water or stock. Bring to boil and simmer for 10 to 15 minutes in pressure cooker, or 15 to 20 minutes if not in pressure cooker.

7. Serve with ground Parmesan cheese.

Note. (Optional) If you don't like the sound of 'beanless' then add a tin of kidney beans, or a tin of baked beans in tomato sauce.

33 Beef Stewed in White Wine

Ingredients	Quantity	Preparation
Bay leaves	2	Crushed
Fresh garlic	2 cloves	Crushed and chopped
Ground black pepper	To taste	
Leek	½	Chopped
Onion	½	Chopped
Salt	To taste	
Shin of beef on the bone	500g/17.5oz/3.3cup	
Stock cube	1	
Sunflower oil	1+1 tablespoon	
Sweet red pepper	½	Chopped
Tomato	1	Chopped
White wine	200ml/1/3pt	
Worcestershire sauce	Dash	

In a frying pan and a large casserole dish.

1. Fry shin of beef in 1 tablespoon of sunflower oil until browned. Remove and put in a casserole dish.

2. Deglaze the frying pan with half the white wine and a dash of Worcestershire sauce, pour the deglazed mixture over the beef.

3. In clean frying pan, fry onion and fresh garlic in 1 tablespoon sunflower oil until it starts to brown.

4. Add leeks and continue frying for 5 minutes.

5. Add chopped tomato, salt and ground black pepper and add remainder of the white wine. Stir.

6. Add all the fried vegetables to casserole, add bay leaves, cover casserole and put in oven on high temperature Gas Mark 8/Electric 230°c/Fan 210°c for 20 minutes.

7. Turn heat down to Gas Mark 1.5/Electric 145°c/Fan 125°c and continue to cook for 3 to 4 hours.

8. Taste and add stock cube. Serve.

34 Curried Liver

Ingredients	Quantity	Preparation
Calves' liver	500g/17.5oz/3.3cup	Cut into small cubes
Coconut oil	1 tablespoon	
Cumin powder	1 teaspoon	
Dark soy sauce	Splash	
Fresh coriander	Bunch	Chopped
Fresh garlic	2 cloves	Crushed and chopped
Lettuce leaves	Few	Chopped
Mustard seeds	1 teaspoon	
Onion	1 small	Chopped
Paprika powder	2 teaspoons	
Peanut butter	2 teaspoons	
Soya milk, milk or water	Splash	
Tomatoes	2	Chopped
Turmeric powder	1 teaspoon	

In a wok or a large pan.
1. Melt coconut oil and fry mustard seeds, 1 minute.
2. Add onion and fresh garlic and fry until the onion is soft.
3. Add tomato, crush and fry until a paste.
4. Add a little dark soy sauce.
5. Add turmeric powder, cumin powder and paprika powder and fry for 3 minutes.
6. Add calves' liver and fry for 10 minutes.
7. Add lettuce leaves and fresh coriander.
8. Add a little soya milk, milk or water.
9. Stir in the peanut butter and serve.

35 Lamb Stock

Ingredients	Quantity	Preparation
Bay leaves	2	Crushed
Bones from roast shoulder of lamb		
Celery	4 sticks	Chopped
Fresh garlic	To taste	
Fresh oregano	Bunch	Chopped
Olive oil	1 tablespoon	
Onion	1	Chopped
Water	1litre/2pints	

In a pressure cooker or large pan.
1. Heat 1 tablespoon of olive oil and fry onion, fresh garlic and celery until onion is brown.
2. Add bones from roast shoulder of lamb, fresh oregano, bay leaves and water, bring to boil, then simmer covered for 10 minutes or 30 minutes if not in pressure cooker.

36 Lambs' Liver Curry

Ingredients	Quantity	Preparation
Cabbage	150g/5.25oz/1cup	Chopped
Chillies (red or green)	2	Chopped
Cumin seeds	½ teaspoon	
Fresh garlic	3–4 cloves	Crushed and chopped
Fresh ginger	1.25cm/½in	Chopped
Ground fenugreek	1 teaspoon	
Lambs' liver	450g/15.75oz/3cup	Chopped finely
Oil	1 tablespoon	
Onion	½	Chopped
Paprika powder	1 teaspoon	
Soy sauce	1 tablespoon	For marinade
Sweet pepper (any)	½	Chopped
Tomato purée	Squirt	
Tomato	1	Chopped
Turmeric powder	1 teaspoon	
Water	Splash	

In a bowl and a wok or large pan.

1. Allow lambs' liver, chopped finely, to marinate for 15 minutes in soy sauce.
2. In the wok or large pan, heat oil and fry onion, fresh garlic, fresh ginger and cumin seeds until onion is translucent.
3. Add chillies, turmeric powder, paprika powder and ground fenugreek and fry for 1 minute.
4. Add tomato, crush and fry until it forms a paste.
5. Add other vegetables (cabbage and sweet pepper) and stir well. Add a little water.
6. Add marinated lambs' liver.
7. Bring to simmer, adding a squirt of tomato purée.
8. Simmer for 10 to 15 minutes until liver is cooked. Serve.

37 Lebanese Style Lamb

Ingredients	Quantity	Preparation
Chilli powder	½-1 teaspoons	Depends on strength and taste
Cinnamon stick	4cm/1.5in	Broken up
Cloves	1 teaspoon	
Courgette	1	Diced
Fresh coriander	Bunch	Diced
Fresh garlic	3 cloves	Crushed and chopped
Ground black pepper	To taste	
Ground cardamom	1 teaspoon	
Minced lamb or chopped raw lamb	500g/17.5oz/3.3cup	
Olive oil	1 tablespoon	
Onion	1 small	Chopped
Salt	To taste	
Soy sauce	Dash	
Sweet orange or yellow pepper	1 small	Deseeded and diced
Tin chopped tomatoes	400g/14oz/2.6cup	

In a wok or a frying pan.

1. Fry onion and fresh garlic in olive oil until onion browns.
2. Add minced lamb or chopped raw lamb and fry until brown.
3. Add spices (chilli powder, ground cardamom, cloves and cinnamon stick), stir in and fry for 2 minutes.
4. Add courgettes and sweet orange or yellow pepper, mix and fry for 1 minute.
5. Add chopped tomatoes, mix in, bring to simmer and stir on heat for 10 minutes.
6. Add a dash of soy sauce.
7. Add a good sprig of chopped fresh coriander, stir in.
8. Serve with salt and ground black pepper to taste.

38 Leftover Roast Beef Chinese Style

Ingredients	Quantity	Preparation
Chilli powder	½ teaspoon	
Dark soy sauce	2 tablespoons	
Fennel bulb	1 large	Halved and sliced finely
Fresh garlic	3 cloves	Crushed and chopped
Green chillies	1	Diced
Leftover cooked roast beef	750g/26oz/5cup	Cut into thin slices
Oil	2 tablespoons	For frying
Onion	1 small	Sliced finely
Sweet green pepper	1	Deseeded and sliced finely
Water	4 tablespoons	

In a wok or large pan.
1. Heat oil and add onions and fry for 2 to 3 minutes.
2. Add sweet green pepper and sliced fennel bulb and continue to fry until fennel starts to soften.
3. Add fresh garlic and green chillies.
4. Add sliced leftover cooked roast beef and chilli powder. Mix altogether.
5. Add dark soy sauce and water. Bring to simmer and continue to cook until beef warmed through.
6. Serve with rice, or Chinese leaf, shredded and blanched and lightly covered with light soy sauce and warmed oil.

39 Leftover Roast Beef Curry

Ingredients	Quantity	Preparation
Butternut squash	½ small	Peeled, deseeded and cut finely
Carrot	1 small	Cut finely
Chillies (red or green)	2 small	Cut finely
Chilli sauce	2 tablespoons	
Dark soy sauce	1 tablespoon	
Fresh garlic	2 cloves	Crushed and chopped
Ground almonds	2 tablespoons	
Leftover beef gravy or red wine	3 tablespoons	
Leftover cooked roast beef	250g/9oz/1.7cup	Cut into small chunks
Madras curry powder	2 teaspoon	
Onion	2	Cut finely
Tomatoes	2 medium	Diced
Vegetable oil	2 tablespoons	
Water	If needed	

In a wok or a large pan.
1. Heat vegetable oil and fry onions gently until transparent.
2. Add fresh garlic and chillies and fry.
3. Add butternut squash and carrots and fry 3 to 4 minutes.
4. Add Madras curry powder tossed through the butternut squash, onion and carrots to coat them and cook for further 1 to 2 minutes.
5. Add tomatoes and dark soy sauce and the leftover cooked roast beef and fry for a further 5 minutes.
6. Add leftover beef gravy or red wine, and chilli sauce, and cover and cook until butternut squash softens. 10 to 15 minutes. Add water if too dry.
7. When squash is soft add ground almonds to soak up any remaining liquid. Serve.

40 Leftover Roast Beef Spicy with Radish

Ingredients	Quantity	Preparation
Bacon fat or other oil	2 tablespoons	
Cumin powder	1 teaspoon	
Fresh garlic	3 cloves	Crushed and chopped
Fresh ginger	1.25cm/½in	Diced finely
Leftover cooked roast beef brisket	300g/10.5oz/2cup	Cut into small pieces
Leftover cooked beef gravy or stock	250ml/½pint	
Onion	½	Diced
Plum tomatoes	2	Roughly chopped
Radishes	6	Top and tail and chop finely
Red chillies	½ large	Sliced
Turmeric powder	1 teaspoon	

In a wok or a deep frying pan.

1. Heat bacon fat or other oil and add onion and fresh ginger. Fry for 5 minutes.

2. Add fresh garlic and red chillies and continue frying for 2 to 3 minutes.

3. Add turmeric powder and cumin powder and fry for 2 to 3 minutes until you can smell the spices.

4. Add plum tomato, crush and cook until tomato is a paste.

5. Add the leftover cooked beef gravy or stock and bring up to the boil.

6. Add the leftover cooked beef brisket and simmer for 5 minutes until warmed through.

7. Add radishes and continue to cook for 1 to 2 minutes to soften.

8. Serve when beef is heated through.

Note. Good with Mock Chestnut or Garlic Butternut Squash

41 Leftover Roast Lamb in Almond

Ingredients	Quantity	Preparation
Almond butter	2 heaped tablespoons	
Almond oil	2 tablespoons	
Celeriac	½ root	Peeled and cut into very thin chips
Dark soy sauce	1 tablespoon	
Fresh coriander	Bunch	Chopped
Fresh garlic	3-4 cloves	Crushed and chopped
Fresh ginger	2.5cm/1in	Diced finely
Green chillies	1	Sliced finely
Groundnut oil	6 tablespoons	
Leftover lamb gravy or stock	200ml/1/3pint	
Leftover cooked lamb shoulder	200-300g/7-10.5oz/1.3-2cup	Sliced thinly
Onion	½	Sliced thinly
Sweet green pepper	1 small	Deseeded and sliced
Tomato	1	Sliced thinly

In a wok or a large pan.

1. In half the groundnut oil, add the onion and fresh ginger and fry to soften the onion.

2. Add fresh garlic and green chillies and continue to fry.

3. Add celeriac and fry to soften.

4. When celeriac is softened add almond butter and almond oil mixed to a paste with remaining groundnut oil. Stir through celeriac thoroughly.

5. Add sweet green pepper and leftover cooked lamb shoulder and mix well. Add leftover lamb gravy or stock.

6. When sweet green pepper has softened, add tomato and cook until tomato becomes soft.

7. Add dark soy sauce and fresh coriander and mix well. Serve.

42 Leftover Roast Lamb Shoulder Jamaican Style

Ingredients	Quantity	Preparation
Cabbage	2-3 leaves	Chopped
Cardamom pods	4	Pods opened and seeds ground
Chillies (red or green)	2	Chopped
Coconut oil	1 tablespoon	
Cumin powder	1 teaspoon	
Fresh coriander	Bunch	Chopped
Fresh garlic	3 cloves	Crushed and chopped
Fresh ginger	2.5cm/1in	Chopped
Fresh thyme	2 teaspoons	
Ground coriander	2 teaspoons	
Ground fenugreek	1 teaspoon	
HP sauce	2 tablespoons	
Leftover lamb gravy or stock	To cover	
Leftover cooked roast lamb shoulder	500g/17.5oz/3.3cup	Cubed
Onion	1	Chopped
Runner beans	Handful	Chopped
Sweet red pepper	1	Deseeded and chopped
Tomatoes	2	Chopped
Turmeric powder	1 teaspoon	
Worcestershire sauce (optional)	Dash	

In a wok or a large pan.
1. Heat the coconut oil and fry onion, fresh garlic and fresh ginger.
2. Add spices (ground coriander, ground seeds from cardamom pods, ground fenugreek, turmeric powder, cumin powder, fresh thyme and chillies) and cook for 2 minutes.
3. Add the leftover cooked roast lamb shoulder, tomatoes, HP sauce and (optional) Worcestershire sauce with leftover lamb gravy or stock to cover.
4. Add the other vegetables (cabbage, runner beans and sweet red pepper).
5. Simmer on low heat for 20 minutes. Add fresh coriander.
6. Serve.

43 Leftover Roast Lamb Spicy Mongolian Style

Ingredients	Quantity	Preparation
Eggs	3	Beaten
Fresh garlic	3 large cloves, or 5 small cloves	Crushed and chopped
Ground black pepper	2 teaspoons	
Lamb dripping or oil	2 tablespoons	
Leftover lamb gravy or stock	1 tablespoon	
Leftover cooked lamb	350g/12oz/2.3cup	Diced
Onion	1 large	Diced
Red chillies	3	Diced
Sweet chill sauce	1 tablespoon	

In a bowl and a wok or large pan.
1. Heat the lamb dripping or oil and add the onion, fresh garlic and red chillies and fry for 2 to 3 minutes.
2. When onion is browned, add leftover lamb gravy or stock, and sweet chilli sauce and warm through.
3. Add leftover cooked lamb and cook until warm, turning frequently.
4. Mix the ground black pepper into the beaten egg and add to the lamb and mix in very quickly.
5. Cook altogether for further 1 minute until egg is cooked.
6. Serve.

44 Moussaka

Ingredients	Quantity	Preparation
Aubergine	1	Sliced and fried
Bay leaves	1	Crushed
Cheddar cheese	100g/3.5oz/0.7cup	Grated
Chillies (red or green)	1	Chopped
Cinnamon powder	1 tablespoon	
Courgette	½	Chopped thinly
Dried oregano	1 tablespoon	
Fresh garlic	4 cloves	Chopped
Ground black pepper	1 tablespoon	
Minced lamb	500g/17.5oz/3.3cup	
Olive oil	1+3 tablespoons	
Onion	1 small	Chopped
Soft cream cheese	50g/1.75oz/0.3cup	
Sun dried tomatoes	5	Chopped
Tin chopped tomatoes	400g/1.4oz/2.6cup	

In a wok or a large pan, frying pan and oven pan.

1. Heat 1 tablespoon olive oil and fry onion, fresh garlic and chillies until onion is starting to brown.
2. Add minced lamb and cinnamon powder and stir until meat is cooked and brown.
3. Add courgettes, tin chopped tomato and sun dried tomatoes, bring to simmer and cook for 15 minutes.
4. Brush aubergine with 3 tablespoons of olive oil and, in separate pan, fry aubergines on both sides, 3 to 4 minutes.
5. Put half the lamb mixture into the large oven pan.
6. Cover lamb mixture with half the fried aubergine slices.
7. Put a little soft cream cheese on each aubergine slice.
8. Repeat the lamb and aubergine layers.
9. Scatter the Cheddar cheese across the top
10. Put in oven at Gas Mark 5/Electric 190°c/Fan 170°c for 15 minutes. Serve.

45 Pork and Aubergine Vindaloo Style Curry

Ingredients	Quantity	Preparation
Aubergine	1	Chopped into cubes
Broccoli	2 florets	Chopped
Chilli powder	1 teaspoon	
Cider vinegar	1 tablespoon	
Cumin seeds	1 teaspoon	
Dark soy sauce	2 teaspoons	For marinade
Fresh coriander	Bunch	Chopped
Fresh garlic	5 cloves	Crushed and chopped
Fresh ginger	1.25cm/½in	Chopped
Mustard seeds	1 teaspoon	
Oil	1 tablespoon	
Onion	1 small	Chopped
Paprika powder	1 teaspoon	
Pork tenderloin	450g/15.75oz/3cup	Cut thinly
Red wine	1 tablespoon	For marinade
Soya milk or milk	Splash	
Tomato	1	Chopped
Turmeric powder	1 teaspoon	

In a bowl and wok or frying pan.
1. Add thinly sliced pork tenderloin to a marinade of a little dark soy sauce and red wine.
2. Heat oil and fry, covered, the onion, cumin seeds, fresh garlic, mustard seeds and fresh ginger for 3 minutes.
3. Add tomato, crush and fry to a paste.
4. Add other spices (chilli powder, turmeric powder and paprika powder) and fry for 3 minutes.
5. Remove pork tenderloin from marinade with slotted spoon, add to fried spice mixture, and fry until it starts to brown.
6. Add aubergine and stir it in, then add broccoli.
7. Add soya milk or milk and cook for 15 minutes, adding more if necessary.
8. Add fresh coriander. Stir in cider vinegar.
9. Serve.

46 Pork and Butternut Squash Curry

Ingredients	Quantity	Preparation
Aubergine	½	Sliced thickly
Butternut squash	½	Deseeded and quartered
Chinese leaf or several Savoy cabbage leaves	Head	Chopped
Coconut oil	1 tablespoon	
Cumin seeds	1 teaspoon	
Dark soy sauce	2 teaspoons	For marinade
Fresh coriander	1 bunch	Chopped
Fresh garlic	2 cloves	Crushed and chopped
Fresh ginger	1.25cm/½in	Chopped
Green chillies	1	Chopped
Light soy sauce	Splash	
Mustard seeds	1 teaspoon	
Olive oil	2+2 tablespoons	
Onion	½	Chopped
Pork tenderloin	450g/15.75oz/3cup	Thinly sliced and marinated
Soya milk or milk	Splash	
Tomato	1	Smashed
Turmeric powder	1 teaspoon	
White wine	1 tablespoon	For marinade

In an oven pan, a bowl, a wok or large pan and frying pan.
1. Cut in half, rub with 2 tablespoons of oil and roast the aubergine and butternut squash for 45 minutes on Gas Mark 6/Electric 200°c/Fan 180°c (or microwave for 15 minutes).
2. Marinate the pork tenderloin in the white wine and dark soy sauce.
3. Heat coconut oil in a wok or large pan, not too hot. Add mustard seeds and cumin seeds. Fry, covered, until they pop.
4. Add onion, fresh garlic, fresh ginger and green chillies and fry until onion starts to brown.
5. Add smashed tomato and turmeric powder, fry until it forms a paste.
6. Remove from marinade with slotted spoon and fry pork separately in 2 tablespoons of olive oil until done, then add to mixture.
7. Add mashed and skinned roast butternut squash and mashed roast aubergine.
8. Add Chinese leaf or savoy cabbage. Mix well.
9. Add a splash of light soy sauce, stir and cook for 15 minutes, adding a splash of soya milk or milk if it gets dry.
10 Serve up sprinkled with chopped fresh coriander.

47 Pork Autumn Curry or Harvest Vindaloo Style Curry

Ingredients	Quantity	Preparation
Bramley apples or cooking apples	1	Peeled, cored and chopped
Carrot	1	Sliced
Cider vinegar	100ml/1/6pint	
Cloves	4-5	
Cumin seeds	1 teaspoon	
Fresh garlic	3+3 cloves	Crushed and chopped
Fresh ginger	1.25cm/½in	Chopped finely
Ground fenugreek	1 teaspoon	
Mustard seeds	1 teaspoon	
Oil	1 tablespoon	
Onion	1	Chopped
Pork tenderloin	400g/14oz/2.6cup	Cut into small chunks
Red chillies	2 (or more)	Chopped
Sugar	½ teaspoon	
Sun dried tomatoes	4	Chopped
Sweet yellow pepper	1 small	Deseeded and chopped
Tomatoes	2	Chopped
Turmeric powder	1 teaspoon	
Water	To cover	Boiling

In a bowl, a wok or large pan.

1. Add the oil and fry the onion, half the fresh garlic, the red chillies, fresh ginger, mustard seeds, cumin seeds and clove until onion is translucent and mustard seeds have popped.

2. Make a paste with half the cider vinegar, ground fenugreek and turmeric powder. Add to mixture and fry for 5 minutes.

3. Add tomatoes and mash to a paste.

4. Add pork tenderloin to mixture with the other half of the fresh garlic and fry for 5 minutes.

5. Add sun-dried tomatoes, sweet yellow peppers, carrot and Bramley apple or cooking apple and stir in, adding boiling water to cover.

6. Cook for 2 hours on slow heat, simmering.

7. Add remaining cider vinegar and sugar, and simmer for 5 minutes. Serve.

48 Pork Mince Balls

Ingredients	Quantity	Preparation
Cinnamon powder	½ teaspoon	
Cloves	4	Ground
Coriander seeds	1 teaspoon	Ground
Eggs	1	Beaten
Fennel seeds	½ teaspoon	Ground
Fresh coriander	Handful	Chopped
Fresh garlic	6 cloves	Crushed and chopped
Green chillies	1	Chopped
Ground ginger	2 teaspoons	
Minced pork	500g/17.5oz/3.3cup	
Oil	1 tablespoon	
Red chillies	1	Chopped
Whole black peppercorns	½ teaspoon	Ground

In pestle, 2 bowls and an oven pan.

1. Grind the different spices (cloves, coriander seeds, fennel seeds and whole black peppercorns), add cinnamon powder and ground ginger, mix and put in bowl with fresh coriander, red chillies, green chillies and fresh garlic.

2. Rub oven pan with oil.

3. Beat egg in bowl.

4. Add minced pork to spice mix and mix well by hand.

5. Add beaten egg.

6. Form into small meatballs, oil hands and turn meatballs in them then place the meatballs on oiled oven pan.

7. Cook at Gas Mark 6/Electric 200°c/Fan 180°c for 30 minutes. Turn halfway through.

8. Serve.

49 Rissoles

Ingredients	Quantity	Preparation
Cumin powder	1 teaspoon	
Dried marjoram or dried oregano	1 tablespoon	
Eggs	1	Beaten
Fresh garlic	1 clove	Chopped finely
Ground almonds	50g/1.75oz/0.3cup	
Ground black pepper	To taste	
Leftover cooked roast meat (venison, beef or lamb)	250g/9oz/1.7cup	Chopped finely or ground
Lemon juice	Splash	
Soya milk or milk or beer or water	Splash	
Oil	For frying	
Onion	1	Chopped finely
Worcestershire sauce	1 tablespoon	

In a mixing bowl and large frying pan.

1. Mix everything (leftover cooked roast meat, ground almonds, beaten egg, onion, fresh garlic, cumin powder, dried marjoram or dried oregano, Worcestershire sauce, lemon juice, ground black pepper and soya milk, milk, beer or water) except the oil together.
2. If mixture is dry, add a little more soya milk, milk, water or beer. If mixture too wet, add a little more ground almonds.
3. Form into balls about 2.5cm/1in across.
4. Flatten them gently.
5. Heat the oil and fry gently for about 4 to 5 minutes per side.
6. Serve.

Note. Add more garlic if troubled by vampires or dentists.

50 Shepherd's Pie with Lamb and Butternut Squash

Ingredients	Quantity	Preparation
Bouillon powder	2 teaspoons	
Butternut squash	1 small	Deseeded and quartered
Celery	2 sticks	Sliced
Cheddar cheese	50g/1.75oz/0.3cup	Grated
Courgette	1 large	Diced finely
Dried mint	1 tablespoon	
Fresh garlic	2 cloves	Crushed and chopped
Minced lamb	500g/17.5oz/3.3cup	
Olive oil	1+2 tablespoon	
Onion	½	Diced
Tin plum tomatoes	400g/14oz/2.6cup	
Tomato purée	2 teaspoons	
Water	Splash	

In a large pan and a roasting pan.

1. Rub a tablespoon of olive oil onto the halved and deseeded butternut squash.
2. Roast the butternut squash Gas Mark 6/Electric 200°c/Fan 180°c for 45 minutes (or microwave for 15 minutes).
3. Fry the diced onion until translucent in 2 tablespoon olive oil.
4. Add the fresh garlic and celery to the onion and continue to fry.
5. Add the minced lamb and fry until it browns.
6. Add courgettes and fry.
7. Add the dried mint, tin plum tomatoes, tomato purée and bouillon powder. Stir to break up the tomato. Add a drop of water and bring to boil.
8. Lower heat and simmer lamb mixture until butternut squash is ready.
9. Grate the cheese.
10. When cooked, remove butternut squash from its skin, mash with a fork and stir in half the grated cheddar cheese.
11. In roasting pan used for the squash, add the mince mixture and top with the cheesy butternut squash and scatter remaining cheddar cheese over the top. Cook at Gas Mark 6/Electric 200°c/Fan 180°c for 20 minutes.
12. Serve.

51 Spicy Beef Stew

Ingredients	Quantity	Preparation
Asparagus	Bunch	Chopped
Bay leaves	2	Crushed
Celeriac	250g/9oz/1.7cup	Chopped
Chilli powder	Pinch	
Chuck steak-beef	500g/175oz/3.3cup	Diced
Cumin powder	1 teaspoon	
Fresh garlic	2 cloves	Crushed and chopped
Leek	½ large	Chopped
Olive oil	1 tablespoon	
Onion	1 small	Chopped
Stock	To cover	
Tomato purée	2 teaspoon	
Tomato	1	Chopped
Worcestershire sauce	Dash	

In a lidded stew pot.

1. Heat the olive oil and sauté the onion and fresh garlic until onion is translucent.

2. Add chuck steak, turn up heat and stir until brown.

3. Add chilli powder, cumin powder and tomato and stir for 3 minutes.

4. Add other ingredients (asparagus, bay leaves, celeriac, leeks, tomato purée, stock and Worcestershire sauce), stir and put lid on.

5. Put into oven and cook on Gas Mark 1/Electric 140°c/Fan 120°c for 4 hours.

6. Serve in bowls, with crusty bread if you are a gannet.

Note. Even better when warmed up the next day.

52 Spicy Dry Chilli Pork

Ingredients	Quantity	Preparation
Chorizo oil or butter	2 tablespoons	
Dark soy sauce	2 tablespoons	For marinade
Fresh garlic	2 cloves	For marinade, crushed and chopped
Fresh ginger	2.5cm/1in	For marinade, diced
Pork tenderloin	500g/17.5oz/3.3cup	Strip off fat and cut into small thin slices
Red chillies	1	For marinade, sliced thinly
Spring onions	3	Sliced thinly
White wine	2 tablespoons	For marinade

In a mixing bowl, and a wok or frying pan.
1. For marinade put white wine, dark soy sauce, fresh garlic, fresh ginger and red chillies together in bowl and mix.
2. Add pork tenderloin, mix and leave to marinate.
3. In frying pan, heat chorizo oil or butter, add pork and marinade and fry until marinade evaporates, 10 minutes.
4. Add spring onions and mix in.
5. Serve with Fresh Garlic, Fennel and Leeks.

POULTRY

53 Chicken Stock

Ingredients	Quantity	Preparation
Bay leaves	1	Crushed
Celery	3-4 sticks	Roughly chopped
Fresh garlic	2 cloves	Crushed and chopped
Olive oil	1 tablespoon	
Onion	½	Roughly chopped
Leftover roast chicken carcasses	1	What is left after a roast has been carved
Leftover roast vegetables (optional)	If any	What is left after a roast dinner
Red chillies	1	Roughly chopped
Water	1litre/2pints	Boiling

In a pressure cooker or a large covered pan.

1. Use the carcass of a previously roasted chicken.

2. Fry all the other ingredients (bay leaves, celery, fresh garlic, red chillies and onion) for 3-5 minutes in olive oil in the base of pressure cooker or large pan.

3. If you have any, then add other vegetables that are left from the roast chicken dinner.

4. Place cooked chicken carcasses in a trivet on top of fried vegetables.

5. Pour over boiling water.

6. Add pressure cooker lid, bring it up to pressure, then lower temperature and leave to cook slowly for 20 minutes or so.

7. When cold, remove chicken carcass and take off any meat.

8. Returned cooked meat to stock and blitz to blend. Alternatively, sieve the stock to remove vegetables and keep cooked meat to add later.

9. If not using pressure cooker. Leave to cook in large covered pan on low heat for 40 minutes.

54 Duck Breast in Gravy

Ingredients	Quantity	Preparation
Bacon fat or a good oil	1 tablespoon	
Chillies (red or green)	1 small	Chopped
Duck breast	1	Cut into strips across the grain
Fresh garlic	3 cloves	Crushed and chopped
Onion	1 small	Sliced
Soy sauce	Dash	For marinade
Wine	200ml/1/3pint	For marinade
Stock or vegetable water or water	125ml/¼ pint	Leftover from cooking any vegetables

In a bowl and a wok or a frying pan.
1. Marinate duck breast in wine and soy sauce for 1 hour.
2. Heat bacon fat or good oil in pan. Add duck breasts removed from marinade with slotted spoon, turning duck to brown the outside and crisp the skin. Save remaining marinade.
3. Add onions and fry for 2 minutes.
4. Add fresh garlic and chillies and fry for 1 minute.
5. Add remaining marinade and the stock, vegetable stock/water or water, or add more wine (if wanted).
6. When the sauce is reduced enough, serve with mixed green vegetables.

55 Leftover Roast Chicken and Bacon Hash

Ingredients	Quantity	Preparation
Chilli-infused olive oil	1 tablespoon	
Fresh garlic	5 cloves	Crushed and chopped
Garlic-infused olive oil	1 tablespoon	
Green beans	50g/1.75oz/0.3cup	Diced
Ground black pepper	2 teaspoons	
Leftover cooked chicken	250g/9oz/1.7cup	Diced
Maple syrup	1 tablespoon	
Onion	1	Sliced
Rocket leaves	50g/1.75oz/0.3cup	
Smoked streaky bacon	6 slices	Chopped
Sweet red pepper	1	Deseeded and sliced

In a wok or large pan.

1. Heat the chilli-infused olive oil and garlic-infused olive oil and fry onion until translucent, 3 to 4 minutes.

2. Add green beans, sweet red pepper and ground black pepper and fry to soften sweet pepper.

3. Add smoked streaky bacon and fresh garlic and fry altogether 2 to 3 minutes.

4. Add leftover cooked chicken and stir through. Fry for a further 2 to 3 minutes until cooked.

5. Add maple syrup and mix through.

6. Add rocket leaves and stir until wilted.

7. Serve.

56 Leftover Roast Chicken and Chorizo Casserole

Ingredients	Quantity	Preparation
Cabbage leaves	1-2	Chopped
Chicken stock	125ml/¼pint	
Chillies (red or green)	1	Chopped
Chorizo sausage	½	Skinned and cut into chunks
Courgette	1	Chopped
Fresh garlic	2 cloves	Crushed and chopped
Leftover cooked chicken	Handful	
Olive oil	1 tablespoon	
Onion	½	Chopped
Peanut butter	1 tablespoon	
Sweet green pepper	1	Deseeded and chopped
Tomato purée	Squirt	

In a casserole or large pan.
1. Fry onion and fresh garlic in olive oil until soft.
2. Add chillies and chorizo sausage and fry for 1 to 2 minutes.
3. Add vegetables (cabbage, courgettes and sweet green pepper). Fry for a few minutes.
4. Add leftover cooked chicken, tomato purée, chicken stock and peanut butter and stir.
5. Simmer for 10 minutes.
6. Serve.

57 Leftover Roast Chicken Curry

Ingredients	Quantity	Preparation
Broccoli	4 florets	Diced
Carrot	1 small	Diced
Chicken stock	200ml/1/3pint	
Coconut oil	2 tablespoons	
Cream	1 tablespoon	
Cumin powder	½ teaspoon	
Dried red chillies	2	Chopped
Fennel seeds	½ teaspoon	
Fresh coriander	Bunch	Chopped
Fresh garlic	3 cloves	Crushed and chopped
Fresh ginger	1.25cm/½in	Diced
Leftover cooked chicken	250g/9oz/1.7cup	Diced
Peas	100g/3.5oz/0.7cup	
Red onion	1	Chopped
Tomato	1	Chopped
Turmeric powder	1 teaspoon	

In a wok or a large pan.
1. Heat the coconut oil and fry red onion, fresh garlic, fresh ginger and dried red chillies until red onion is translucent.
2. Add spices (cumin powder, fennel seeds and turmeric powder) and cook until you can smell the spices.
3. Add tomatoes, crush and cook to a paste.
4. Add leftover cooked chicken and vegetables (broccoli, carrots and peas) and fry for 5 minutes.
5. Add chicken stock. Stir.
6. Cook until vegetables are soft.
7. Add fresh coriander.
8. Add cream and stir in.
9. Serve.

58 Leftover Roast Chicken Curry 2

Ingredients	Quantity	Preparation
Black mustard seeds	1 teaspoon	
Brussels sprouts	6	
Chillies (red or green)	1	Chopped
Coconut oil	2 tablespoons	
Cumin seeds	1 teaspoon	
Fresh coriander	1 Bunch	Chopped
Fresh garlic	2 cloves	Crushed and chopped
Fresh ginger	1.25cm/½in	Chopped
Ground almonds	1 tablespoon	
Leek	½	Chopped
Leftover cooked chicken	500g/17.5oz/3.3cup	Cubed
Onion	1	Chopped
Peanut butter	1 tablespoon	
Soy sauce	Dash	
Soya milk or milk	125ml/¼pint	
Sweet yellow pepper	½	Deseeded and chopped
Tomatoes	2	Chopped

In a wok or large pan.
1. Heat coconut oil, add black mustard seeds and cumin seeds, and fry on moderate heat for 2 to 3 minutes.
2. Add onion, fresh garlic, fresh ginger and chillies and fry for 5 minutes.
3. Add tomatoes, crush and fry until a smooth paste.
4. Add remaining vegetables (Brussels sprouts, leek and sweet yellow pepper) and stir.
5. Add leftover cooked chicken and stir in.
6. Add soya milk or milk and simmer for 10 minutes.
7. Add fresh coriander, ground almonds, peanut butter and soy sauce and stir.
8. Simmer for 5 minutes, adding more liquid if it sticks.
9. Serve with rice or naan bread.

59 Leftover Roast Chinese Style Chicken

Ingredients	Quantity	Preparation
Dark soy sauce	2 tablespoons	
Fresh garlic	3 cloves	Crushed and chopped
Fresh ginger	2.5cm/1in	Chopped finely
Green chillies	1	Chopped finely
Groundnut oil	2 tablespoons	
Leek	½	Chopped finely
Leftover cooked chicken	300g/10.5oz/2cup	Chopped into strips
Onion	1	Chopped very finely
Spring onions	2	Chopped finely
Sweet green pepper	1	Deseeded and chopped finely
Tomatoes	2	Chopped finely
White, elderberry or other fruit wine	2 tablespoons	

In a wok or large pan.

1. Heat groundnut oil and fry onion for 2 to 3 minutes until browned.
2. Add fresh garlic, fresh ginger and sweet green pepper and fry 2 to 3 minutes.
3. Add green chillies, leek, spring onions, tomatoes and fry 2 to 3 minutes.
4. Add leftover cooked chicken and fry to warm through.
5. Sprinkle over dark soy sauce and white wine or elderberry wine or other fruit wine and fry for 2 to 3 minutes to reduce liquid a little.
6. Serve.

60 Lemon Chicken Curry

Ingredients	Quantity	Preparation
Chicken breasts	590g/21oz/4cup	Skinned and diced small
Chillies	1 small	Diced
Fresh coriander	Handful	Diced
Fresh garlic	3 cloves	Crushed and chopped
Ground black pepper	½ teaspoon	
Lemon juice	2 tablespoon	For marinade
Madras curry powder	1 teaspoon	
Romaine lettuce	½	Sliced
Salt	Pinch	
Sunflower oil	1 tablespoon	
White onion	1 small	Sliced

In a bowl, a wok or large pan.
1. Mix lemon juice and diced chicken breasts and marinate for 2 to 3 minutes.
2. Heat sunflower oil and fry white onion gently to soften, 2 to 3 minutes.
3. Add chillies and Madras curry powder and fry until you can smell the spice.
4. Add chicken breasts, fresh garlic and salt and ground black pepper and fry 4 to 5 minutes or until chicken is cooked.
5. Add romaine lettuce and chopped fresh coriander and stir well and cook for a further 2 to 3 minutes to soften lettuce (depending upon lettuce type.
6. Serve.

61 Paprika Turkey

Ingredients	Quantity	Preparation
Celery	100g/3.5oz/0.7cup	Chopped
Dark soy sauce	1 teaspoon	
Dried red chillies	4 small	Diced
Fresh ginger	5cm/2in	Diced
Ground black pepper	1 teaspoon	
Kale	100g/3.5oz/0.7cup	Chopped
Lettuce leaves	8	Chopped
Paprika powder	2 teaspoons	
Salt	½ teaspoon	
Sunflower oil	150ml/1/4pint	
Turkey mince	500g/17.5oz/3.3cup	
Water	200ml/1/3pint	

In a wok or a large pan.
1. Heat the sunflower oil and fry fresh ginger and dried red chillies for 1 minute.
2. Add the turkey mince and fry until brown.
3. When brown, add paprika powder and mix well to cover turkey.
4. Add celery, kale and water. Bring to simmer and cook 3 to 5 minutes.
5. Add lettuce leaves and stir through with ground black pepper, salt and dark soy sauce.
6. Serve with rice or naan bread.

62 Scotch Eggs

Ingredients	Quantity	Preparation
Eggs	1	Beaten
Ground almonds	150g/5.25oz/1cup	
Ground linseed	50g/1.75oz/0.3cup	
Ground nutmeg (optional)	½ teaspoon	
Groundnut oil	200-300ml/1/3-½pint	
Hard boiled eggs	5	Peeled
Oil	Splash	
Pork sausage meat	500g/17.5oz/3.3cup	
Turmeric powder (optional)	1 teaspoon	

In a mixing bowl, small bowls, a wok or deep frying pan and a roasting pan.

1. Hard boil 5 eggs. Allow to cool and peel.
2. Split pork sausage meat into 5 lots, flatten each on palms of hands, then wrap 1 lot tightly around 1 egg, smoothing and evening the surface. Repeat for each egg.
3. Turn the covered egg in the ground linseed (optionally mixed with the ground nutmeg), covering all areas.
4. Turn each in beaten egg, covering all areas.
5. Turn each in ground almonds (optionally mixed with turmeric powder), covering completely.
6. Repeat for each egg.
7. In a deep pan, heat groundnut oil and drop in the covered eggs. Fry, until the outside is browned, turning to ensure even colour.
8. When all browned put into oven in a pan, with a little oil to prevent sticking, at Gas Mark 6/Electric 200°c/Fan 180°c for 25 minutes.
9. Allow to cool.

63 Smoky Red Hot Chicken

Ingredients	Quantity	Preparation
Cherry tomatoes	140g/5oz/1cup	Cut in half
Chicken breasts	300g/10.5oz/2cup	Cut into thin strips
Dried red chillies	2 small	Diced
Fresh garlic	5 cloves	Crushed and chopped
Green Padron peppers	70g/2.5oz/½cup	Sliced thinly
Mustard seeds	1 teaspoon	
Smoked paprika powder	1 teaspoon	
Red onion	1 small	Sliced
Soft cream cheese	100g/3.5oz/0.7cup	
Sunflower oil	1 tablespoon	

In a wok or a large pan.

1. Heat the sunflower oil and fry the red onion to soften it, 3 to 4 minutes.
2. Add dried red chillies, fresh garlic and mustard seeds and fry 1 to 2 minutes.
3. Add chicken breasts and cook to brown the outside, turning frequently.
4. Add smoked paprika powder and mix well. Continue frying 1 to 2 minutes.
5. Add halved cherry tomatoes and green Padron pepper and mix well. Fry 1 to 2 minutes.
6. Add soft cream cheese and mix in well, cook for a further 2 to 3 minutes, turning frequently to prevent sticking.
7. Serve.

64 Spanish Style Chicken Stir-fry

Ingredients	Quantity	Preparation
Chicken breasts	2	Skinned and cubed
Chilli sauce	1.5 tablespoons	For marinade
Chorizo sausage	½	Skinned and sliced thinly
Leek	½	Slice thinly
Olive oil	2 tablespoons	
Onion	½	Slice thinly
Paprika powder	2 teaspoons	
Truffle oil	1 teaspoon	

In a wok or a large pan.
1. Marinate chicken breasts in chilli sauce.
2. Fry onion and leeks in olive oil for 3 minutes.
3. When onion and leeks cooked, add chicken breasts in the chilli sauce and cook for 3 minutes or until chicken pieces are browned.
4. Add paprika powder and chorizo sausage mix and continue to fry until chicken is cooked.
5. Before serving, drip truffle oil over and mix in.
6. Serve with green salad.

65 Spiced Duck

Ingredients	Quantity	Preparation
Chilli powder	¼ teaspoon	
Courgette	1	Chopped finely
Cumin powder	1 teaspoon	
Duck breasts	2	Sliced thinly
Fresh garlic	1 clove	Chopped finely
Fresh ginger	2.5cm/1in	Chopped finely
Onion	½	Chopped finely
Soy sauce	1 tablespoon	For marinade
Sunflower oil	1 tablespoon	
Sweet yellow pepper	1 small	Deseeded and sliced finely
Tomato purée	1 tablespoon	
Water	As needed	
White wine	2 tablespoons	For marinade

In a bowl and a wok or frying pan.
1. Marinate duck breasts in white wine and soy sauce for 30 minutes to an hour.
2. Heat sunflower oil and fry onion, fresh garlic, fresh ginger, chilli powder and cumin powder until onion is starting to brown.
3. Add courgettes and sliced sweet yellow pepper.
4. Add duck breasts removed from marinade with slotted spoon and cook until they are no longer pink.
5. Add a little of the marinade and a little water.
6. Simmer for 15 minutes.
7. Serve.

66 Sweet Ginger Chicken

Ingredients	Quantity	Preparation
Celery	3 sticks	Sliced finely and cut into 1.25cm/½in strips
Chicken breasts	3	Cut into small thin strips
Coconut oil	2 tablespoons	
Courgette	1	Cut into thin strips of 4cm/1.5in
Dark soy sauce	2 tablespoons	For marinade
Fresh garlic	3 cloves	Crushed and chopped
Fresh ginger	4cm/1.5in	Chopped finely
Onion	½	Sliced finely
Rapeseed oil	1 tablespoon	
Red chilli	1	Cut into small discs
Red wine	2 tablespoons	For marinade
Sweet chilli sauce	1 tablespoon	For marinade
Sweet green pepper	1	Deseeded and cut into thin strips

In a bowl and a wok or frying pan.

1. Put chicken breasts into a marinade of red wine, dark soy sauce and sweet chilli sauce.
2. Heat the rapeseed oil and coconut oil and add the onion and fry for 3 to 4 minutes.
3. Add fresh garlic and fresh ginger and fry for 1 to 2 minutes.
4. Add sweet green pepper, celery and courgettes and red chillies and fry for 4 to 5 minutes.
5. Take chicken from marinade with slotted spoon and add to pan. Fry until chicken cooked through, 5 to 8 minutes.
6. Add any remaining marinade and heat through, reducing until sauce thickens.
7. Serve with steamed asparagus.

GAME

67 Cajun Style Pheasant

Ingredients	Quantity	Preparation
Cayenne chilli powder	1 teaspoon	
Cumin powder	1 teaspoon	
Dried oregano	1 teaspoon	
Fresh garlic	2 cloves	Grated
Ground mixed pepper, black and white	1.5 teaspoons	
Oil	1 tablespoon	
Onion	¼	Grated
Paprika powder	1.5 teaspoons	
Pheasant breasts	2	Skinned and diced
Water	Splash	

In a heavy frying pan.

1. Mix all the spices (cayenne chilli pepper, cumin powder, dried oregano, ground mixed pepper, paprika powder, fresh garlic and onion) together.

2. Remove pheasant breast from pheasant and skin them.

3. Flatten the pheasant breasts a little with palm of hand or flat of a knife.

4. Rub a little oil over the breasts.

5. Coat both sides with spice mix.

6. Heat heavy frying pan with no oil until a drop of water sizzles.

7. Add pheasant breasts, fry for 2 to 3 minutes per side, ensuring good ventilation.

8. Serve with Celeriac Dauphinoise and roasted peppers or a salad.

68 Pigeon Stock

Ingredients	Quantity	Preparation
Bay leaves	1	Crushed
Carrot	1	Roughly chopped
Celery	2 sticks	Roughly chopped
Fresh garlic	2 cloves	Crushed and chopped
Olive oil	1 tablespoon	
Pigeon carcasses	2	Roasted with breasts removed
Red chilli	1	Roughly chopped
Red onion	½	Roughly chopped
Water	750ml/1.5pint	

In a roasting pan and pressure cooker or large covered pan.
1. Roast the pigeon carcasses for 20 minutes, Gas Mark 5/Electric 190°c/Fan 170°c.
2. When cooked, (if not done before roasting) remove the pigeon breasts and set aside (for Quick Pigeon in Wine or Pigeon Mulligatawny Soup).
3. Fry all the other ingredients (bay leaves, carrots, celery, fresh garlic, red chillies and red onion) for 3-5 minutes in olive oil in the base of the pressure cooker or large pan.
4. Place roasted pigeon carcasses in a trivet and place on top of fried vegetables.
5. Pour over boiling water.
6. Add pressure cooker lid, bring it up to pressure, then lower temperature and leave to cook slowly for half an hour or so. (If not using pressure cooker, leave to simmer in large covered pan on low heat for 1 to 2 hours.)
7. When cold, remove pigeon carcass and take off any meat.
8. Return cooked meat to stock and blitz to blend. Alternatively, sieve the stock to remove vegetables and keep cooked meat to use later.

69 Quick Pigeon in Wine

Ingredients	Quantity	Preparation
Butter or bacon fat	1 tablespoon	
Celery	2 sticks	Chopped
Cloves	3	
Courgette	1	Cut into strips and diced
Double cream	2 tablespoons	
Fennel seeds	2 teaspoons	
Fresh garlic	2 cloves	Crushed and chopped
Fresh ginger	2.5cm/1in	Diced
Mushrooms	200g/7oz/1.3cup	Diced
Pigeon breast	2	Cut thinly
Plum tomatoes	2 diced	
Red onion	½	Diced
Rosé wine or any wine	2 tablespoons	For marinade
Soy sauce	1 teaspoon	For marinade
Sweet green pepper	½	Deseeded and diced
Tomato purée	2 teaspoons	

In a wok.

1. Marinate pigeon breasts in soy sauce and 2 tablespoons of rosé wine or any wine.

2. Fry red onion, fresh garlic, sweet green pepper and fresh ginger together in butter or bacon fat on low heat for 5 minutes.

3. Add courgettes, mushrooms, and celery and fry until all soft.

4. When vegetables are soft add plum tomato and mix.

5. Make a well in middle, and taking pigeon out of marinade, add to well and stir to fry, browning both sides.

6. Mix all together, add marinade and additional wine if necessary. Add tomato purée, cloves and fennel seeds and simmer for 10 minutes.

7. Take off heat. Add double cream, stir and serve.

70 Venison Steaks in Pepper Sauce and Greens

Ingredients	Quantity	Preparation
Butter	Knob	
Broccoli	Large	Broken in florets
Double cream	1 tablespoon	
Leek	1	Chopped
Oil	1 tablespoon	
Shallot	1	Chopped
Venison steaks	2	Well-coated with black pepper
Water	Splash	
White wine	Shot glass	
Whole black peppercorns	1 tablespoon	Roughly ground

In a pan and a frying pan.

1. Put chopped leeks in a pan with melted butter and cook covered on a low heat.
2. Blanche the broccoli florets, saving the water. Add broccoli to leeks and stir regularly.
3. Add shallots.
4. Heat frying pan with a little oil. Cover venison steaks on both sides with roughly ground whole black pepper and fry in oil, turning once.
5. When vegetables and steak are done, plate up steaks and vegetables.
6. Add a shot glass of white wine to frying pan to deglaze and stir to take up juices from the venison steaks.
7. Add a splash of water from the blanching.
8. When boiling, add double cream.
9. Poor warmed double cream mixture over steaks.
10. Serve.

71 Winter Warming Venison Stir-fry

Ingredients	Quantity	Preparation
Chilli sauce	1 tablespoon	For marinade
Cloves	6	Ground
Courgette	1	Diced
Dark soy sauce	2 tablespoons	For marinade
Fresh garlic	2 cloves	Crushed and chopped
Fresh ginger	2.5cm/1in	Chopped finely
Leek	½	Sliced and diced
Oil	2 tablespoons	
Red chillies	2	Chopped
Red onion	½	Sliced finely
Tomato purée	1 tablespoon	
Venison steak	350g/12oz/2.3cup	Diced small
Whole black peppercorns	9	Ground

In a bowl and a wok or large pan.

1. Marinate diced venison steaks in dark soy sauce and chilli sauce.

2. While meat is in the marinade, heat oil, fry red onion, red chillies, fresh ginger and fresh garlic and fry for 1 to 2 minutes.

3. Add ground whole black peppercorns and ground cloves and stir through.

4. Spoon venison from marinade, add to red onions and stir. Fry for 4 to 5 minutes, stirring.

5. Add courgettes and leeks and remaining marinade sauce. Stir. Fry for 4 to 5 minutes.

6. Add tomato purée. Stir thoroughly.

7. Serve.

FISH

72 Baked Courgette Nest with Salmon

Ingredients	Quantity	Preparation
Cayenne chilli	1	Diced
Courgettes	1 large or 2 small	Sliced thinly
Fresh garlic	6 cloves	Crushed and chopped
Ground black pepper	1 teaspoon	
Oil	1.5 tablespoons	
Paprika powder	2 teaspoons	
Salmon steaks	260g/9oz/1.7cup	Skinned and cut into strips
Water	As required	

In a bowl and an oven pan.

1. Slice the courgettes using a potato peeler or similar and scatter in an oiled oven pan.
2. Scatter fresh garlic and cayenne chilli pepper over the courgettes and mix together.
3. Add the little water.
4. In the bowl, mix oil, paprika powder and ground black pepper and turn the salmon steaks in it.
5. Add salmon steaks to oven pan and toss it all altogether.
6. Cover with cooking foil and bake Gas Mark 6/Electric 200°c/Fan 180°c for 30 minutes.
7. Serve piled into a nest with liquid from roasting pan poured around it.

73 Baked Sea Bass

Ingredients	Quantity	Preparation
Courgette	½	Sliced thinly
Oil	1-2 teaspoons	
Onion	1 small	Sliced thinly
Rosemary butter	2 tablespoons	
Sea bass or white fish fillets	4 fillets, 400g/14oz/2.6cup	
Sweet red pepper	½	Deseeded and chopped

In a roasting pan.
1. Oil the pan.
2. Put onion, courgettes, sweet red pepper into pan.
3 Place sea bass or white fish fillets on top.
4. Add generous knob of rosemary butter on top of fish.
5. Cover with cooking foil.
6. Cook Gas Mark 6/Electric 200°c/Fan 180°c for 30 minutes.
7. Serve with Garlic Spinach.

74 Baked Sole

Ingredients	Quantity	Preparation
Chillies (red or green)	1	Chopped
Courgette	1	Chopped
Fresh garlic	1 clove	Chopped
Olive oil	Drizzle	
Onion	½	Chopped
Sole fillets or white fish fillets	3-4	
Sweet red pepper	½	Deseeded and chopped
Tomato	1	Slices

In a roasting pan.
1. Add vegetables (courgettes, onion and sweet red pepper) to roasting dish except for tomato and chillies.
2. Layer sole fillets or white fish fillets on top.
3. Layer tomato, fresh garlic and chillies on top.
4. Drizzle with olive oil.
5. Cover with cooking foil and cook at Gas Mark 6/Electric 200°c/Fan 180°c for 40 minutes.
6. Serve with juice from pan poured over the top. Good with buttered leeks.

75 Buttered Smoked Haddock

Ingredients	Quantity	Preparation
Butter	3 tablespoons	
Carrots	50g/1.75oz/0.3cup	Diced very small
Ground black pepper	To taste	
Leek	210g/7.5oz/1.5cup	Diced
Salt	To taste	
Smoked haddock or smoked white fish	250g/9oz/1.7cup	Skinned and diced
Sweet green pepper	70g/2.5oz/½cup	Deseeded and diced
Tomatoes	200g/7oz/1.3cup	Diced

In a wok or a large pan.
1. Heat butter and when melted add leeks, sweet green pepper and carrot and cook until starting to soften, 4 to 5 minutes.
2. Add tomato and smoked haddock or other smoked white fish. Mix well and cook until fish warmed through, 3 to 4 minutes.
3. Add salt and ground black pepper to taste.
4. Serve.

76 Creamy Fish and Mushrooms

Ingredients	Quantity	Preparation
Courgette	1 small	Diced small
Fresh garlic	4 cloves	Crushed and chopped
Ground black pepper	1 teaspoon	
Mushrooms	200g/7oz/1.3cup	Chopped
Oil	1 tablespoon	
Red chillies	1 small	Diced
Soft cream cheese	100g/3.5oz/0.7cup	
Smoked haddock or smoked white fish	350g/12oz/2.3cup	Skinned and chopped small
Tin chopped tomatoes	400g/14oz/2.6cup	
Tomato purée	Squirt	
White onion	1 small	Chopped

In a wok or a large pan.
1. Heat the oil and fry white onions to soften, 2 to 3 minutes.
2. Add fresh garlic and fry to soften, 1 to 2 minutes.
3. Add mushrooms, mix well and fry for 3 to 4 minutes.
4. Add courgettes and red chillies and mix well.
5. Add tin chopped tomatoes, tomato purée and ground black pepper, mix well.
6. Add smoked haddock or other smoked white fish and bring to simmer and cook for 2 to 3 to 4 minutes.
7. Add soft cream cheese. Mix in well and cook further 2 minutes.
8. Serve.

77 Curried Whole Fish

Ingredients	Quantity	Preparation
Cumin powder	2 teaspoons	
Double cream	2 tablespoons	
Fresh garlic	6–8 cloves	Crushed and chopped
Garlic-infused olive oil	2 tablespoons	
Ground almonds	200g/7oz/1.3cup	
Red chillies	2	Diced
Smoked haddock or smoked white fish	4 pieces	
Turmeric powder	2 teaspoons	
Vinegar	2 teaspoons	
Water	To cover	

In a large pan and a wok or large pan.
1. Mix vinegar and water in a flat pan and add smoked haddock or other smoked white fish and poach for 5 minutes.
2. In a separate pan, heat the garlic-infused olive oil and add the fresh garlic and red chillies and fry for 2 to 3 minutes.
3. Add cumin powder and turmeric powder to garlic and chillies and fry for a further 2 to 3 minutes.
4. Add ground almonds and double cream to the spices and mix together, heating through.
5. When fish is cooked, place on plate and cover with the thick creamy sauce.
6. Serve with wilted spinach.

78 Fried Fish and Chinese Style Sauce

Ingredients	Quantity	Preparation
Fresh garlic	5 cloves	Crushed and chopped
Fresh ginger	1.25cm/½in	Diced finely
Ground linseed	30g/1oz/0.2cup	
Hake or other white fish	250g/9oz/1.7cup	
Light soy sauce	1 tablespoon	
Paprika powder	1 teaspoon	
Red chillies	2 small	Cut finely
Red wine	4 tablespoons	
Salmon steaks	250g/9oz/1.7cup	
Spring onions	4	Cut thinly lengthwise
Sunflower oil	6 tablespoons	
Sweet chilli sauce	2 tablespoons	

In a bowl and a wok or large pan.
1. Cut salmon steaks and the hake or other white fish into 1.25cm/1in strips and turn in a mixture of ground linseed and paprika powder.
2. Heat sunflower oil and add both types of fish in small batches. Deep fry each batch until cooked, 3 to 4 minutes. Remove to a warm plate.
3. Remove all except 2 tablespoons of oil from the pan, put fresh garlic, fresh ginger, red chillies and spring onions in and fry for 1 minute.
4 Add sweet chilli sauce, light soy sauce and red wine and warm through.
5. Plate a mixture of the cooked pieces of salmon and hake or other white fish and pour hot sauce over.
6. Serve with rice or a rocket salad.

79 Italian Style Hake Curry

Ingredients	Quantity	Preparation
Coconut oil	3 tablespoons	
Cavolo nero or cabbage	100g/3.5oz/0.7cup	Chopped
Cumin seeds	1 teaspoon	
Fresh coriander	Bunch	Roughly chopped
Fresh garlic	1-2 cloves	Crushed and chopped
Green chillies	1	Chopped
Hake or other white fish	400g/14oz/2.6cup	Cut into cubes
Mascarpone cheese	100g/3.5oz/0.7cup	
Mustard seeds	1 teaspoon	
Paprika powder	1 teaspoon	
Soy sauce	Dash	
Soya milk or milk	Dash	
Spring onions	1	Chopped
Tomato	1 small	Chopped
Turmeric powder	1 teaspoon	

In a wok or a large pan.

1. Heat coconut oil and spring onion, fresh garlic and green chillies and fry for 3 minutes.

2. Add other spices (cumin seeds, mustard seeds, turmeric powder and paprika powder) and fry for 2 minutes.

3. Add tomato, crush and fry until it makes a paste.

4. Add cavolo nero or cabbage and fry for 1 minute.

5. Add hake or other white fish, mix and fry for 1 minute.

6. Add soya milk or milk, and soy sauce and cook until fish is ready.

7. Add Mascarpone cheese and stir in.

8. Add fresh coriander and stir in.

9. Serve.

80 Lime Cream Tuna and Spicy Greens

Ingredients	Quantity	Preparation
Coconut oil	1 tablespoon	
Courgette	1	Diced
Cumin seeds	2 teaspoons	
Fresh garlic	4-6 cloves	Crushed and chopped
Ground black pepper	½ teaspoon	
Lime juice	1 tablespoon	
Mustard seeds	2 teaspoons	
Oil	1+1 tablespoon	
Red chillies	4 small	Diced
Red onion	1	Thinly sliced
Sour cream	2 tablespoons	
Spring cabbage	2 leaves	Remove spine and cut finely
Tuna steak	400g/14oz/2.6cup	
Turmeric powder	1 teaspoon	

In a wok or a large pan, frying pan and saucepan.

1. Heat coconut oil in 1 tablespoon of any other oil and fry red onions to soften.

2. Add fresh garlic, red chillies, mustard seeds, cumin seeds and turmeric powder and fry gently for 1 to 2 minutes.

3. Add courgettes and spring cabbage and fry gently for 2 to 3 minutes.

4. Add tuna steaks to a different frying pan in 1 tablespoon of oil and fry gently, turning once.

5. Mix sour cream and lime juice and cook together in another pan, add ground black pepper.

6. After 3 to 4 minutes cooking the tuna, serve with the spiced greens and pour over the cream sauce.

81 Pepper Mushroom Fish Curry

Ingredients	Quantity	Preparation
Chillies (red or green)	1 small	Diced
Courgettes	600g/21oz/4cup	Diced
Fresh garlic	4 cloves	Crushed and chopped
Ground black pepper	½ teaspoon	
Madras curry powder	1 teaspoon	
Mushrooms	350g/12oz/2.3cup	Diced small
Onion	1 small	Diced
Smoked haddock or smoked white fish	200g/7oz/1.3cup	Skinned and diced
Soft cream cheese	100g/3.5oz/0.7cup	
Sunflower oil	1.5 tablespoons	
Whole black peppercorns	2 teaspoons	

In a wok or a large pan.

1. Heat the sunflower oil and fry the onion to soften, 2 to 3 minutes.
2. Add fresh garlic and chillies and fry for 1 to 2 minutes.
3. Add Madras curry powder and mix well and fry for 1 to 2 minutes.
4. Add mushrooms and fry for 3 to 4 minutes.
5. Add ground black pepper and whole black peppercorns. Mix well.
6. Add courgettes and cook to soften for 3 to 4 minutes.
7 Add smoked haddock or other smoked white fish and soft cream cheese. Mix well and cook for 4 to 5 minutes.
8. Serve.

82 Sardine and Pilchard Curry

Ingredients	Quantity	Preparation
Coconut oil	1 tablespoon	
Cumin seeds	½ teaspoon	
Fresh garlic	3 cloves	Crushed and chopped
Fresh ginger	2.5cm/1in	Chopped
Green chillies	1	Chopped
Ground coriander	1 teaspoon	
Leek	1	Cut finely
Mustard seeds	½ teaspoon	
Onion	1	Chopped
Soya milk or milk or water	As needed	
Tin pilchards	600g/21oz/4cup	Drained
Tin sardines	300g/10.5oz/2cup	Drained
Tomatoes	2	Chopped
Turmeric powder	1 teaspoon	

In a wok or large pan.

1. Fry cumin seeds and mustard seeds in coconut oil until they start to pop.

2. Add onions and fresh ginger, fresh garlic and green chillies and fry until the onion is translucent.

3. Add tomatoes, ground coriander and turmeric powder, frying, and squashing to form a paste.

4. Add leeks and mix in.

5. Add drained tins of pilchards and sardines, breaking them up and stirring in.

6. Add soya milk, milk or water to keep it moist. Simmer for 5 minutes.

7. Serve.

83 Smoked Haddock Curry

Ingredients	Quantity	Preparation
Cabbage	¼	Chopped
Caraway seeds	½ teaspoon	
Chillies	1	Chopped
Coconut oil	1 tablespoon	
Cumin seeds	1 teaspoon	
Fresh coriander	Bunch	Chopped
Fresh garlic	3 cloves	Crushed and chopped
Fresh ginger	1.25cm/½in	Chopped
Mustard seeds	1 teaspoon	
Oil	1 tablespoon	
Onion	1 small	Chopped
Paprika powder	2 teaspoons	
Peanut butter	1 teaspoon	
Smoked haddock or smoked white fish	400g/14oz/2.6cup	Skinned, cut into 1.25cm/½in strips
Soy sauce	Dash	
Sweet green or red pepper	½	Deseeded and chopped
Soya milk or milk or water	Splash	
Tomato	1	Chopped
Turmeric powder	1 teaspoon	

In a wok or a large pan.
1. Melt coconut oil in tablespoon of another oil, add caraway seeds, mustard seeds and cumin seeds. Fry for 1 minute until seeds start popping.
2. Add onion, fresh garlic, fresh ginger and chillies and fry until onion is translucent.
3. Add paprika powder and turmeric powder and fry for 1 minute.
4. Add tomato and stir, crushing it until it forms a paste.
5. Add a little cabbage and sweet red or green pepper and cook for 5 minutes.
6. Add soy sauce and a little soya milk, milk or water to prevent sticking.
7. Add smoked haddock or other smoked white fish and cook for 5 minutes.
8. Stir in peanut butter and chopped fresh coriander.
9. Serve.

84 Smoked Haddock in Piquant Textured Sauce

Ingredients	Quantity	Preparation
Butternut squash	1 small	Deseeded and quartered
Cabbage	200g/7oz/1.3cup	Chopped finely
Fresh garlic	3 cloves	Crushed and chopped
Ground black pepper	To taste	
Olive oil	1+1 tablespoon	
Onion	1	Chopped finely
Red chillies	1	Chopped finely
Salt	To taste	
Soft cream cheese	100g/3.5oz/0.7cup	
Smoked haddock or smoked white fish	2	Skinned and chopped
Tomato	1	Sliced thinly and chopped
White wine vinegar	1 teaspoon	
Water	As required	

In a wok or a large pan, and an oven pan.

1. Rub 1 tablespoon of olive oil onto the halved and deseeded butternut squash halves.
2. Roast the butternut squash Gas Mark 6/Electric 200°c/Fan 180°c for 45 minutes (or microwave for 15 minutes).
3. Heat 1 tablespoon of the olive oil and fry the onion and fresh garlic until it starts to brown.
4. Add the red chillies and fry for another minute.
5. Add cabbage and fry for a further 5 minutes, stirring often.
6. Stir in mashed roasted butternut squash.
7. Add soft cream cheese and stir in. Add a little water if it starts to stick.
8. Heat up smoked haddock or other smoked white fish by either poaching in a pan of water with a dash of white wine vinegar or heating in the microwave in a little water.
9. Put fish on plate.
10. Add white wine vinegar to sauce. Season with salt and ground black pepper.
11. Stir in the chopped raw tomato.
12. Spoon sauce over fish.
13. Serve.

85 Spicy Tomato Fish Stew

Ingredients	Quantity	Preparation
Carrots	100g./3.5oz/0.7cup	Diced
Cavolo nero leaves, cabbage or other dark greens	50g/1.75oz/0.3cup	Diced
Chillies (red or green)	2 small	Diced
Fennel seeds	2 teaspoons	
Fresh garlic	4 cloves	Crushed and chopped
Fresh ginger	2.5cm/1in	Diced
Ground black pepper	1 teaspoon	
Haddock or other white fish	300g/10.5oz/2cup	Diced
Olive oil	1 tablespoon	
Onion	1	Sliced
Salt	To taste	
Tin chopped tomatoes	400g/14oz/2.6cup	
Tin sweetcorn	150g/5.25oz/1cup	Drained

In a wok or a large pan.

1. Heat the olive oil and fry onion for 3 minutes.
2. Add fresh garlic, chillies and fresh ginger and fry 1 to 2 minutes.
3. Add carrots and fennel seeds and fry 2 to 3 minutes.
4 Add cavolo nero or cabbage or other dark greens and haddock or other white fish and mix in.
5. Add tin of chopped tomatoes and tin of sweetcorn and mix well.
6. Cover and simmer for 20 minutes, stirring occasionally.
7. Add salt and ground black pepper to taste.
8. Serve.

86 Sweetcorn Cod

Ingredients	Quantity	Preparation
Broccoli	250g/9oz/1.7cup	Well chopped
Cod or other white fish	250g/9oz/1.7cup	Skinned and diced
Fresh basil	Handful	Chopped
Fresh garlic	4 cloves	Crushed and chopped
Herby roulade cheese	100g/3.5oz/0.7cup	
Oil	1 tablespoon	
Onion	1	Diced
Tin sweetcorn	150g/5.25oz/1cup	Drained
Water	2 tablespoons	

In a wok or a large pan.
1. Heat the oil and fry onion for 2 to 3 minutes to soften.
2. Add fresh garlic, broccoli and tin of sweetcorn and mix well.
3. Add water and cook to soften broccoli for 3 to 4 minutes.
4. Add herby cheese roulade and mix in, allowing it to melt.
5. Add cod or other white fish pieces and mix in gently. Cover and heat for 2 to 4 minutes until fish is cooked.
6. Add fresh basil.
7. Serve.

87 White Fish Curry

Ingredients	Quantity	Preparation
Butter	25g/1oz/0.2cup	
Double cream	200ml/1/3pint	
Cod, coley, haddock, pollock or other white fish	300g/10.5oz/2cup	Skinned
Fresh garlic	6 cloves	Crushed and chopped
Fresh ginger	2.5cm/1in	Diced
Green chillies	2	Diced
Ground almonds	100g/3.5oz/0.7cup	
Onion	1	Diced
Soya milk or milk	100ml/1/6pint	
Spinach	100g/3.5oz/0.7cup	
Turmeric powder	2 teaspoons	

In a wok or a large pan.
1. Melt butter and fry onions until softened.
2. Add green chillies, fresh garlic and fresh ginger and fry for 2 minutes.
3. Add turmeric powder and fry until you can smell the spice, 1 to 2 minutes.
4. Add ground almonds, soya milk or milk, double cream and heat to boil.
5. Add cod, coley, haddock, pollock or other white fish and simmer for 5 to 10 minute.
6. Break up the fish and add spinach. Cook for further 2 to 3 minutes.
7. Serve.

88 Whole Cauliflower and Fish Curry

Ingredients	Quantity	Preparation
Cauliflower	500g/17.5oz/3.3cup or 1 small whole	
Cod or other white fish	250g/9oz/1.7cup	Skinned and diced
Fresh garlic	4 cloves	Crushed and chopped
Fresh ginger	2.5cm/1in	Diced
Madras curry powder	1 teaspoon	
Oil	1 tablespoon	
Soft cream cheese	100g/3.5oz/0.7cup	
Thai red chillies	1	Diced
Turmeric powder	2 teaspoons	
Water	200ml/1/3pint	

In a wok or a large pan.

1. Separate the leaves from the cauliflower.
2. Blitz the cold cauliflower florets into grains.
3. Cut cauliflower stem from leaves and chop very finely.
4. Roughly chop the leaves.
5. Heat the oil and gently fry fresh garlic, Thai red chillies and fresh ginger.
6. Add turmeric powder and Madras curry powder and fry until you can smell the spice.
7. Add diced cauliflower stems and cook for 2 minutes.
8. Add cauliflower leaves and cook 1 to 2 minutes. Turn frequently to avoid burning.
9. Add blitzed cauliflower grains and soft cream cheese. Mix well.
10. Add 200ml of water and mix well.
11. Add cod or other white fish and stir in. Simmer for 8 to 10 minutes. Add more water if required. Stir constantly.
12. Heat until cauliflower and fish are cooked. Serve.

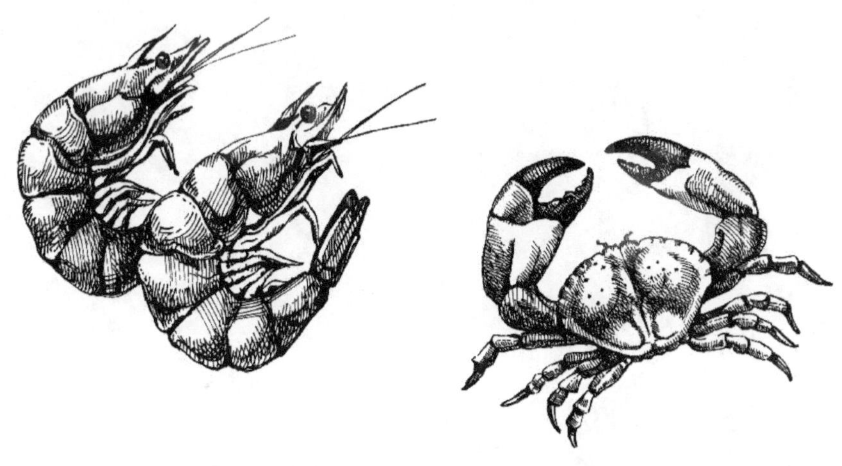

SHELLFISH

89 Celery Prawns

Ingredients	Quantity	Preparation
Carrots	2 small	Diced
Celery	5 sticks	Diced
Chillies (red or green)	1 small	Diced
Coconut oil	1 tablespoon	
Cucumber	2.5cm/1in	Diced
Fresh garlic	4 cloves	Crushed and chopped
Fresh ginger	2.5cm/1in	Diced
Iceberg lettuce	¼	Diced
Onion	1 small	Diced
Paprika powder	1 teaspoon	
Prawns	220g/8oz/1.5cup	Pre-cooked and peeled
Sour cream	3 tablespoons	
Soy sauce	1 tablespoon	
Sweet green pepper	½	Deseeded and diced
Sunflower oil	1 tablespoon	
Tomato	1	Diced

In a wok or a large pan.

1. Melt coconut oil into sunflower oil. Add onion and fry 2 to 3 minutes.
2. Add fresh garlic, fresh ginger, chillies and paprika powder and fry 1 minute.
3. Add tomato and fry to soften for 3 to 4 minutes.
4. Add soy sauce and mix in.
5. Add cucumber, sweet green pepper, carrot, celery and iceberg lettuce and fry 4 to 5 minutes.
6. Add prawns and fry 4 to 5 minutes.
7. Add sour cream and heat through.
8. Serve.

90 Cheese Roulade Prawns

Ingredients	Quantity	Preparation
Carrots	300g/10.5oz/2cup	Thinly sliced lengthwise with vegetable peeler
Fresh basil	Bunch	Chopped
Herby cheese roulade	100g/3.5oz/0.7cup	
Onion	1	Chopped
Prawns	325g/11.5oz/2.25cup	Pre-cooked and peeled
Sweet green pepper	25g/1oz/0.2cup	Deseeded and diced
Sunflower oil	1 tablespoon	
White cabbage	150g/5.25oz/1cup	Sliced thinly

In a wok or a large pan.

1. Heat the sunflower oil and fry onion gently until soft, 2 to 3 minutes.

2. Add white cabbage and sweet green pepper and continue to fry 3 to 4 minutes.

3. Add carrots and herby cheese roulade. Stir to melt the cheese.

4. When melted, add the prawns, stir well and cook 5 to 8 minutes until carrots and prawns are cooked.

5. Add fresh basil and stir through.

6. Serve.

91 Chinese Style Prawns

Ingredients	Quantity	Preparation
Chilli powder	¼ teaspoon	
Coconut or sunflower oil	2 tablespoons	
Dark soy sauce	1 tablespoon	
Fresh garlic	2 cloves	Crushed and chopped
Fresh ginger	4cm/1½in	Diced
Prawns	500g/17.5oz/3.3cup	Pre-cooked and peeled
Spring onions	3	Cut into thin slices
Sweet red pepper	1	Deseeded and sliced
Tomato purée	1 tablespoon	
White wine	3 tablespoons	

In a wok or a large pan.
1. Heat coconut oil or sunflower oil and add fresh garlic and fresh ginger. Fry for 1 to 2 minutes.
2. Add spring onion and sweet red pepper and fry to soften the red pepper for 1 to 2 minutes.
3. Add white wine and tomato purée, mix well.
4. Add dark soy sauce and heat through.
5. When mixture is boiling, add prawns and chilli powder. Stir well to coat the prawns. Cook for 3 to 5 minutes.
6. Serve with rice or Chinese leaf, shredded and blanched and lightly covered with light soy sauce and warmed oil.

92 Cream Cheese Prawn Curry

Ingredients	Quantity	Preparation
Chillies (red or green)	1	Diced
Cumin powder	1 teaspoon	
Fresh garlic	5 cloves	Crushed and chopped
Fresh ginger	2.5cm/1in	Diced
Green Padron peppers	70g/2.5oz/½cup	Diced
Leek	1 small	Diced
Onion	1 small	Sliced
Prawns	325g/11.5oz/2.25cup	Pre-cooked and peeled
Salt	Pinch	
Soft cream cheese	100g/3.5oz/0.7cup	
Sunflower oil	1.5 tablespoons	
Tomatoes	4	Diced
Turmeric powder	2 teaspoons	

In a wok or a large pan.

1. Heat the sunflower oil and fry the onion to soften, 2 to 3 minutes.
2. Add chillies, fresh ginger and fresh garlic and fry 1 to 2 minutes.
3. Add leeks and green Padron peppers and fry, turning frequently, 2 to 3 minutes.
4. Add cumin powder and turmeric powder and mix well.
5. Add tomato and a pinch of salt. Turn frequently, fry 3 to 4 minutes.
6. Add prawns and mix well. Cook 3 to 5 minutes.
7. Add soft cream cheese and mix in well. Continue cooking 2 to 3 minutes.
8. Serve.

93 Creamed Red Prawns

Ingredients	Quantity	Preparation
Beetroot	380g/13.5oz/2.5cup	Diced small
Celery	1 stick	Diced
Fresh garlic	4 cloves	Crushed and diced
Oil	1 tablespoon	
Prawns	300g/10.5oz/2cup	Pre-cooked and peeled
Red chillies	2 small	Diced
Red onion	1	Thinly sliced
Sour cream	150g/5.25oz/1cup	
Spinach	Handful	Diced
Sweet red pepper	1	Deseeded and diced

In a wok or a large pan.
1. Heat the oil and fry the red onion for 3 to 4 minutes.
2. Add fresh garlic, red chillies, sweet red pepper and celery and fry to soften 2 to 3 minutes.
3. Add beetroot and cook, turning frequently, 2 to 3 minutes.
4. Add prawns and mix well. Cook for a further 3 to 4 minutes before adding sour cream and mixing well.
5. Simmer for a further 10 to 15 minutes until beetroot softened.
6. Add spinach, mix well and cook further 1 to 2 minutes.
7. Serve.

94 Creamy Spiced Prawns

Ingredients	Quantity	Preparation
Coconut oil	3 tablespoons	
Crème fraîche	3 tablespoons	
Cumin powder	1.5 teaspoons	
Double cream	3 tablespoons	
Fresh garlic	3 cloves	Crushed and chopped
Fresh ginger	1.25cm/½in	Diced finely
Green chillies	1 small	Chopped finely
Ground coriander	1 teaspoon	
Groundnut oil	1.5 tablespoon	
Leek	100g/3.5oz/0.7cup	Diced finely
Prawns	400g/14oz/2.6cup	Pre-cooked and peeled
Turmeric powder	1.5 teaspoons	
Yellow mustard seeds	1 teaspoon	

In a wok or a large pan.
1. Put all spices (fresh garlic, fresh ginger, green chillies, yellow mustard seeds, ground coriander, cumin powder and turmeric powder) into coconut oil and groundnut oil and fry until yellow mustard seeds starts to pop.
2. Add leeks and continue to fry until it starts to brown, 3 to 4 minutes.
3. Add drained prawns and fry for 5 minutes.
4. Add double cream and crème fraîche and mix well and warm through for 1 to 2 minutes.
5. Serve.

95 Dark Green and Prawn Curry

Ingredients	Quantity	Preparation
Chillies (red or green)	2 small	Diced
Courgette	1 large	Diced
Cumin powder	½ teaspoon	
Dark soy sauce	1 tablespoon	
Fresh garlic	5 cloves	Crushed and chopped
Fresh ginger	2.5cm/1in	Diced
Ground black pepper	1 teaspoon	
Leek	1	Diced
Onion	1 small	Diced
Prawns	180g/6.5oz/1.25cup	Pre-cooked and peeled
Rocket leaves	60g/2oz/0.4cup	Diced
Sweet yellow pepper	1	Deseeded and diced
Turmeric powder	1 teaspoon	
Vegetable oil	2 tablespoons	

In a wok or a large pan.
1. Heat the vegetable oil and fry onion to soften, 2 to 3 minutes.
2. Add fresh garlic, chillies and fresh ginger and fry 2 minutes.
3. Add the leeks and fry for 2 to 3 minutes.
4. Add turmeric powder, cumin powder and ground black pepper and fry until you can smell the spice.
5. Add courgettes, sweet yellow pepper, prawns and dark soy sauce and cook for 5 minutes.
6. Add rocket leaves and simmer for 5 to 10 minutes.
7. Serve.

96 Green and White Prawn Curry

Ingredients	Quantity	Preparation
Broccoli	150g/5.25oz/1cup	Stems removed then chopped finely, chopped florets
Chillies	1	Diced
Curry powder	2 teaspoons	
Double cream	3 tablespoons	
Dried oregano	¼ teaspoon	
Fresh garlic	5 cloves	Crushed and chopped
Fresh ginger	2.5cm/1in	Diced
Ground black pepper	¼ teaspoon	
Leek	1 small	Diced
Onion	1 small	Diced
Prawns	360g/12.5oz/2.5cup	Pre-cooked and peeled
Salt	Pinch	
Sour cream	3 tablespoons	
Sunflower oil	1.5 tablespoons	
White cabbage leaves	150g/5.25oz/1cup	Diced

In a wok or a large pan.
1. Heat sunflower oil and fry onions to soften, 2 to 3 minutes.
2. Add leeks, fresh garlic, chillies, curry powder and fresh ginger and fry 2 to 3 minutes.
3. Add prawns, white cabbage leaves and broccoli stems and cook for 5 to 8 minutes.
4. Add broccoli florets and cook 3 to 4 minutes.
5. Add salt and ground black pepper.
6. Add the double cream and sour cream and stir and heat through.
7. Serve with sprinkled dried oregano.

97 Paprika Prawns

Ingredients	Quantity	Preparation
Chillies	1 small	Diced
Courgette	350g/12oz/2.3cup	Diced
Fresh garlic	4 cloves	Crushed and chopped
Fresh ginger	2.5cm/1in	Diced
Onions	100g/3.5oz/0.7cup	Diced
Paprika powder	2 teaspoons	
Prawns	360g/12.5oz/2.5cup	Pre-cooked and peeled
Soft cream cheese	100g/3.5oz/0.7cup	
Sunflower oil	1.5 tablespoons	
Tomato purée	Squirt	

In a wok or a large pan.

1. Heat the sunflower oil and onion in pan and fry 2 to 3 minutes to soften the onion.
2. Add fresh ginger, fresh garlic and chillies and fry 2 to 3 minutes.
3. Add paprika powder and mix well.
4. Add courgettes, mix well and fry 2 to 3 minutes.
5. Add prawns, mix well and fry 3 to 4 minutes.
6. Add tomato purée and mix through.
7. Add soft cream cheese and mix well. Cook further 2 to 3 minutes.
8. Serve.

98 Prawn and Tuna Curry

Ingredients	Quantity	Preparation
Cabbage leaves	Several	Shredded
Coconut oil	1 tablespoon	
Courgette	1	Chopped
Cumin seeds	1 teaspoon	
Fresh coriander	Bunch	Chopped
Fresh garlic	2 cloves	Smashed
Fresh ginger	1.25cm/½in	Shredded
Ground coriander	1 teaspoon	
Mustard seeds	1 teaspoon	
Prawns	400g/14oz/2.6cup	Pre-cooked and peeled
Red chillies	1	Sliced
Red onion	1 small	Diced
Tomato	1	Smashed
Turmeric powder	2 teaspoons	
Tin tuna	125g/4.5oz/0.8cup	Drained
Water	As required	

In a wok or large pan.

1. Heat coconut oil and fry mustard seeds and cumin seeds until they pop.
2. Add red onion and red chillies and fry for 2 minutes, then add fresh ginger and fresh garlic, and continue frying until starting to brown.
3. Add smashed tomato. Fry until it forms a paste.
4. Add turmeric powder and ground coriander. Fry for 1 minute.
5. Add prawns, courgettes and cabbage leaves and a little water.
6. Add tuna and simmer for 10 minutes.
7. Add fresh coriander leaves and serve.

99 Prawn Curry

Ingredients	Quantity	Preparation
Celery	1 stick	Chopped
Coconut oil	3.5 tablespoons	
Fresh coriander	Bunch	Chopped
Fresh garlic	2 cloves	Crushed and chopped
Green cabbage	¼	Chopped
Light soy sauce	Splash	
Paprika powder	1 teaspoon	
Prawns	350g/12oz/2.3cup	Pre-cooked and peeled
Red chillies	1	Chopped
Shallot	1	Chopped
Salt	To taste	
Sweet green pepper	½	Deseeded and chopped
Tomato	1	Chopped
Turmeric powder	1 teaspoon	
Water	If required	

In a wok or a large pan.

1. Heat coconut oil and fry shallot, celery, fresh garlic and red chillies for 5 minutes until shallot is starting to brown.
2. Add turmeric powder and paprika powder and fry for 2 to 3 minutes.
3. Add tomato, crush and fry until a paste.
4. Add sweet green pepper and green cabbage, mix in and fry for 5 minutes.
5. Add prawns and stir-fry for 5 minutes. Add water if needed.
6. Add fresh coriander and fry for 1 minute.
7. Serve, sprinkle salt and/or light soy sauce, to taste.

100 Red Prawn Curry

Ingredients	Quantity	Preparation
Cumin powder	1 teaspoon	
Fresh garlic	5 cloves	Crushed and chopped
Groundnut oil	2 tablespoons	
Prawns	400g/14oz/2.6cup	Pre-cooked and peeled
Red chillies	2 small	Diced finely
Sweet red pepper	1	Deseeded and sliced thinly
Tomatoes	2	Chopped roughly
Turmeric powder	½ teaspoon	

In a wok or a large pan.
1. Heat groundnut oil and fresh garlic, red chillies and sweet red peppers and fry for 1 to 2 minutes.
2. Add cumin powder and turmeric powder and fry for 1 minute.
3. Add tomatoes, crush and fry until tomatoes are a paste, 2 to 3 minutes.
4. Add prawns and fry until cooked, 3 to 5 minutes.
5. Serve with Mock Chestnut or Garlic Butternut Squash or rice.

101 Sweet Chilli Prawns

Ingredients	Quantity	Preparation
Carrots	200g/7oz/1.3cup	Diced
Chestnut mushrooms	200g/7oz/1.3cup	Diced
Dried red chillies	2	Diced
Fresh ginger	2.5cm/1in	Diced
Green Padron peppers	50g/1.75oz/0.3cup	Diced
Nectarines	2	De-stoned and sliced
Prawns	360g/12.5oz/2.5cup	Pre-cooked and peeled
Sunflower oil	1.5 tablespoons	
Thai red chillies	1 small	Diced

In a wok or a large pan.
1. Heat fresh ginger and Thai red chillies in sunflower oil, 1 to 2 minutes.
2. Add chestnut mushrooms and cook until softened.
3. Add green Padron peppers and carrots and mix well and cook 4 to 5 minutes.
4. Add nectarines and soften on heat 3 to 4 minutes.
5. Add prawns and cook 5 to 8 minutes.
6. Serve.

102 Thai Style Crab Meat and Garlic with Cabbage

Ingredients	Quantity	Preparation
Chilli-infused olive oil	1 teaspoon	
Coconut oil	1 tablespoon	
Fresh garlic	6 cloves	Crushed and chopped
Garlic-infused olive oil	1 teaspoon	
Leek	½	Cut finely
Lemongrass	2 teaspoons	Cut finely
Mange tout	100g/3.5oz/0.7cup	Chopped
Red chillies	2	Cut finely
Savoy cabbage leaves strips	300g/10.5oz/2cup	Spine removed, cut into strips
Savoy cabbage spines	Taken from leaves	Cut very finely
Tin coconut milk	400g/14oz/2.6cup	
Tin white crab meat	240g/8.5oz/1.6cup	Drained
Vegetable oil	1 tablespoon	
White onion	1 large	Cut into strips

In 2 large pans.

1. Heat the vegetable oil, add savoy cabbage leave strips, half the white onion and half the fresh garlic and cook gently.

2. In second pan add coconut oil, leeks, mange tout, savoy cabbage spines, half the white onion, half the fresh garlic, red chillies and lemongrass and mix and fry for 1 to 2 minutes.

3. To the second pan add the coconut milk and bring to simmer for 5 minutes.

4. Add tin of white crab meat to the second pan and cook for 5 minutes.

5. Stir garlic-infused olive oil through savoy cabbage strips in first pan.

6. Stir chilli-infused olive oil through crab meat mixture in second pan.

7. Serve together.

DESSERT

103 Andy's Emergency Almond Steamed Sponge Pudding

Ingredients	Quantity	Preparation
Baking powder	2 teaspoons	
Butter	125g/4.5oz/0.8cup	
Eggs	3	Beaten
Ground almonds	200g/7oz/1.3cup	
Sugar or sugar substitute	6 teaspoons	
Vanilla essence	2 teaspoons	

In a microwaveable bowl.
1. Soften the butter in the microwave for 30 seconds.
2. Add vanilla essence to butter and stir.
3. Add ground almonds and mix well.
4. Add baking powder and sugar or sugar substitute and mix well.
5. Add beaten eggs and mix well.
6. Cover with microwave-proof cling film and microwave for 5 minutes. Check that when a knife is inserted into the centre it comes out clean, otherwise microwave for a further 1 minute and test again (and repeat as necessary depending upon size of eggs used).
7. Serve with cream and sweetened lemon juice, jam or syrup.

104 Mrs G's Boozy Mince Pies

Makes 24 mince pies.

Ingredients	Quantity	Preparation
Pastry		
Butter	250g/9oz/1.7cup	Softened in microwave 20-30 seconds
Eggs	2 small	Beaten
Icing sugar	170g/6oz/1.2cup	Sieved
Lemon	1	Zested
Plain flour	500g/17.5oz/1.2cup	Sieved
Soya milk or milk	2 tablespoons	
Vanilla essence	3 drops	
Mincemeat		
Cinnamon powder	1 tablespoon	
Cloves	12	Ground
Cognac or brandy	150ml/¼pint	
Dried red chillies (optional)	2 small	Ground
Fresh ginger	5cm/2in	Diced
Ground nutmeg	3 teaspoons	
Lemon	1	Zest and juiced
Mixed fruit and peel	500g/17.5oz/3.3cup	
White peppercorns	5	Ground

In 3 mixing bowls and individual cake baking pan.

1. Mix mincemeat ingredients (cloves, fresh ginger, ground cinnamon, ground nutmeg, lemon zest, mixed fruit and peel, ground white peppercorns and (optional) dried red chillies) with the lemon juice and cognac or brandy and leave for 1 to 2 days. Check if drying out and top up with cognac or brandy as necessary.

2. Sieve and combine the plain flour and icing sugar into second bowl and mix in melted butter.

3. Add lemon zest and vanilla essence to beaten egg in a third bowl then add to the flour mixture in second bowl and mix quickly and gently.

4. Roll mixture into a ball, cover and chill for 30 minutes.

5. Using a rolling pin, roll out the mixture then cut out bases and lids for 24 pies.

6. Put bases into baking pan inside cup-cake cases and blind-bake at Gas Mark 4/Electric 180°c/Fan 160°c for 5 minutes with baking beans inside another cup-cake case placed on top of the base pastry in each.

7. Remove baking beans and their cases and bake pastry bases again without beans for 5 more minutes.

8. Add mincemeat mixture to each. Soften the top edge of the base with soya milk or milk and press on lids. Cut 2 small holes in top of each with a knife.

9. Bake for 20 minutes.

105 Mrs G's Pancakes with Almonds

Makes 12 to 16 pancakes.

Ingredients	Quantity	Preparation
Pancakes		
Baking powder or bicarbonate of soda	1.5 teaspoons	
Butter or oil	As required	
Dried egg powder	3-4 tablespoons	
Ground almonds	200g/7oz/1.3cup	
Soya milk or milk	250ml/½pint	
Sugar or sugar substitute	3 tablespoons	
Vanilla essence	1 tablespoon	
Topping		
Double cream	As wanted	
Lemon juice	2 tablespoons	
Sugar or sugar substitute	3 tablespoons	

In a bowl, a jug and a frying pan.
1. Mix dried egg powder, ground almonds, 3 tablespoons of sugar or sugar substitute, and baking powder or bicarbonate of soda together.
2. Add vanilla and half the soya milk or milk. Mix well.
3. Add remaining soya milk or milk and mix well.
4. In a separate jug make the topping: mix 3 tablespoons of sugar or sugar substitute and lemon juice.
5. Heat the butter or oil, in batches, add individual tablespoons of the dried egg powder and ground almond pancake mixture, cooking for 3-4 minutes per side on a low heat.
6. Serve pancakes with a teaspoon of the lemon mixture over them and add a dollop of double cream.

Note. Pancakes can also be served with jam and cream, or syrup and cream.

PICKLE

106 Sweet Pungent Pickle Windfall Apple and Greengage

Makes 3 one pound jars of pickle.

Ingredients	Quantity	Preparation
Bramley apples or cooking apples	350g/12oz/2.3cup	Cored and chopped
Coriander seeds	½ teaspoon	
Dried Thai red chillies	2 small	Chopped
Fresh garlic	7 cloves	Crushed and chopped
Fresh ginger	1.25cm/½in	Diced
Green Thai chillies	2 small	Chopped
Greengages	900g/32oz/6cup	Deseeded and chopped
Ground black pepper	1 teaspoon	
Malt vinegar	250ml/½pint	
Red onion	1	Diced
Salt	1 teaspoon	
White sugar	500g/17.5oz/3.3cup	

In a pressure cooker or a large pan.
1. Add 2 tablespoons of malt vinegar to pan, add spices (coriander seeds, dried Thai red chillies, fresh garlic, fresh ginger, green Thai chillies and ground black pepper) and heat.
2. Add red onion and cook to soften, 2 to 3 minutes.
3. Add Bramley apples or cooking apples and continue to cook, adding more malt vinegar to prevent drying out.
4. Add the greengages and remaining vinegar.
5. Add the white sugar. Bring to the boil, then continue on rolling boil until it starts to change colour (becoming dark brown).
6. While still hot, put into jars. Makes about 3 one pound jars.

Suggestions for *Unhuman* Meals

Andy narrates the *Unhuman* series and gives descriptions of a number of meals, largely cooked by the incomparable Mrs Goodfellow. The following lists food mentioned in the series, and gives, where possible, an appropriate matching recipe in this book that might have inspired it.

For instance Casserole recipe 33 is *Beef Stewed in White Wine* on page 45, casserole recipe 56 is *Leftover Roast Chicken and Chorizo Casserole* on page 76.

<u>Try these recipe numbers</u>

<u>Inspector Hobbes and the Blood:</u>

Casserole	33,56
Cheese & pickle sandwiches	106
Chicken curry & chapattis	57,58,60
Chicken soup	4,10
Cream of chicken soup	4
Stew (police station)	33,51,85

<u>Inspector Hobbes and the Curse:</u>

Beef & mixed salad	17
Beef rissoles	49
Cauliflower cheese	23
Chicken in the bucket	56
Chicken soup	4,10
Crispy salad & dressing	17,18,19
Meat & salad	16,17,18,19
Mulligatawny soup	7
Potage du jour (restaurant)	1,2,3,5,7,8,9,10,11,12,13
Shephard's pie with leftovers	50

<u>Inspector Hobbes and the Gold Diggers:</u>

Cheese & pickle sandwiches	106
Curry (pub)	23,45,46,47,60,77,79,
	81,82.83,87,88,92,95,

	Try these recipe numbers
Curry (pub) continued	96,98,99,100
Pancakes	105
Pork vindaloo	45,47
Stew (camping)	33,51,85

<u>Inspector Hobbes and the Bones:</u>
Beef supper	31,32,33,38,39,40,51
Chicken soup	4,10
Egg & cheese salad	14
Stir fired pork & stuff	45,46,47,52
Stir fried pork, onion & ginger	45,46,47,52

To further whet your appetite, here are the other dishes mentioned in the *Unhuman* books by Wilkie Martin.

<u>Inspector Hobbes and the Blood:</u>
A spread (ham & mustard sandwiches, cheese & pickle sandwiches, cucumber sandwiches, salmon paté sandwiches, cheese, cold tongue, homemade pickles, cream & sherry trifle, coffee cake, dark fruit cake, tinned pears), Bacon & egg, Bacon, eggs & mushrooms, Cottage pie, Crumpets, Doughnuts, Gingerbread, Liver & bacon casserole, Rabbit stewed in cider, Sirloin of beef with fiery horseradish, crispy roast potatoes & parsnips & Yorkshire puddings & cabbage & gravy, Steak & kidney pudding, Sturgeon, Swan, Tea & toast, The best rice pudding in the Universe, Toast & marmalade.

<u>Inspector Hobbes and the Curse:</u>
Bacon & chutney sandwiches, Bacon & eggs, Bang-bang chicken & salad, Beef & mustard sandwiches, Bite-sized meat pies, Caterpillar salad, Cheese sandwiches, Cheese soufflé, Crispy fish & chips, Crusty ham sandwiches, Fillet of Venison & Confit of Shoulder with Dry Fruits Sauce (restaurant), Fish & chips (shop), Fruit cake, Gazpacho soup, Hot dog & onions (van), Jacket potato & cheese, Macaroni cheese, Mushroom omelette, Onion & tomato spiced relish, Oxtail soup, Pea & ham soup,

Pieds de Cochon Farci au Foie Gras et aux Langoustines
(restaurant), Rib-eye steaks & onions, Scrambled eggs, Shank
of Pork Confit with Lentils Sauce & Bacon (restaurant), Steak
& kidney pies (pub), Succulent cold meats, Toast & marmalade.

Inspector Hobbes and the Gold Diggers:
Apple dumplings, Bacon & eggs, Beef & oyster pie, Beef
wellington & horseradish sauce, Blackberry & apple pie,
Borscht (Sid's), Bread, cheese pickle & salad (camping), Cake,
Cheese & chutney sandwiches, Chilli con carne (pub), Fresh eel
(camping), Fried trout & leaves (camping), Full English
breakfast (Sid's), Hamburgers & French fries, Hare (camping),
Kippers (Andy's mum's), Lasagne (Andy's mum's and the cause
of indigestion), Meat pie (camping), Oxtail soup, Rabbit
(camping), Raspberry mousse (Sid's), Roast apple (camping),
Roast belly of pork, mashed potatoes. glazed carrots, peas &
apple sauce, Sorenchester hotpot, Toad in the hole & gravy,
Toast & marmalade.

Inspector Hobbes and the Bones:
Baked beans on toast (Andy's), Beef slow-braised in Hedbury
Stout, creamed potatoes & glazed carrots, Celeriac dauphinoise
& mutton chops, Cheese & onion roll (Golums Logons), Chicken
pie, buttered greens & leeks, Creamy fish chowder, English
sponge, Fried bacon, eggs & fried bread, Full English breakfast,
toast & marmalade, Golden pea soup, croutons & garlic bread,
Porridge, Rich & hearty soup of winter vegetables, basil &
chunks of Italian sausage, with crusty bread, Roast pork,
pointy cabbage, leeks & broccoli & roast dahlia roots (not
recommended), Slow cooked beans & bacon, Smoked haddock
soufflé with herb champ, Sorenchester Old Spot sausages,
mushrooms & scrambled eggs, Sponge cake (Golums Logons),
Toast & marmalade, Trifle.

Abbreviations, Measures and Approximate Equivalents

	Abbreviation	Measure
Weight	g	gram
	cup	cup
	oz	ounce
Measure	cm	centimetre
	in	inch
Quantity	l	litre
	ml	millilitre
	pt	pint

The approximate equivalents that are used in the recipes			Standard equivalents if you want to be more accurate		
Grams	Ounces	American Cups	Grams	Ounces	American Cups
15	0.5	0.1	15	0.53	0.1
20	1	0.13	20	0.7	0.13
25	1	0.2	25	0.88	0.17
30	1	0.2	30	1.05	0.2
50	1.75	0.3	50	1.75	0.33
60	2	0.4	60	2.1	0.4
70	2.5	0.5	70	2.45	0.47
100	3.5	0.7	100	3.5	0.67
125	4.5	0.8	125	4.38	0.83
140	5	1	140	4.9	0.93
150	5.25	1	150	5.25	1
170	6	1.2	170	5.95	1.13
180	6.5	1.25	180	6.3	1.2
200	7	1.3	200	7	1.33
210	7.25	1.5	210	7.35	1.4
220	8	1.5	220	7.7	1.47
240	8.5	1.6	240	8.4	1.6
250	9	1.7	250	8.75	1.67
260	9	1.7	260	9.1	1.73
300	10.5	2	300	10.5	2
325	11.5	2.25	325	11.38	2.17
340	12	2.25	340	11.9	2.27
350	12	2.3	350	12.25	2.33
360	12.5	2.5	360	12.6	2.4
380	13.5	2.5	380	13.3	2.53
400	14	2.6	400	14	2.67

The approximate equivalents that are used in the recipes			Standard equivalents if you want to be more accurate		
Grams	Ounces	American Cups	Grams	Ounces	American Cups
450	15.75	3	450	15.75	3
500	17.5	3.3	500	17.5	3.33
590	21	4	590	20.65	3.93
600	21	4	600	21	4
750	26.25	5	750	26.25	5
800	28	5.3	800	28	5.33
900	32	6	900	31.5	6

The approximate equivalents that are used in the recipes		Standard equivalents if you want to be more accurate	
ml	pints	ml	pints
100	1/6	100	0.17
125	¼	125	0.22
150	¼	150	0.26
200	1/3	200	0.35
250	½	250	0.44
300	½	300	0.52
750	1½	750	1.32

The approximate equivalents that are used in the recipes		Standard equivalents if you want to be more accurate	
cml	in	cm	in
1.25	½	1.25	0.49
2.5	1	2.54	1
4	1.5	4	1.57
5	2	5	1.97
7	3	7	2.76

<u>Oven temperatures used:</u>
Gas Mark 1/Electric 140°c/Fan 120°c
Gas Mark 1.5/Electric 145°c/Fan 125°c
Gas Mark 4/Electric 180°c/Fan 160°c
Gas Mark 5/Electric 190°c/Fan 170°c
Gas Mark 6/Electric 200°c/Fan 180°c
Gas Mark 8/Electric 230°c/Fan 210°c

<u>Spoon measurements used</u>
1 teaspoon about 5ml
1 tablespoon about 15ml

Index

Index is by page number